Information Technology Sector-Specific Plan

An Annex to the National Infrastructure Protection Plan

2010

Homeland Security

Preface

During the past year, members of the Information Technology (IT) Government Coordinating Council (GCC) and the IT Sector Coordinating Council (SCC) collaborated to develop the 2010 IT Sector-Specific Plan (SSP). The IT SSP details the progress the IT Sector has made in its national-level risk management efforts, including the completion of the IT Sector Baseline Risk Assessment (ITSRA) in 2009, and discusses how it is using the results of that baseline analysis to inform the sector's critical infrastructure and key resources (CIKR) protective programs, research and development, and measurement activities.

Other accomplishments since the release of the original SSP in 2007 include:

- The sector developed an approach that provides the basis for sector partners to make informed decisions to avoid, mitigate, tolerate, or transfer national-level IT Sector risks.

- The sector provided leadership to the Cross-Sector Cyber Security Working Group, assisting other CIKR sectors with cybersecurity concerns.

- The sector conducted and participated in domestic and international exercises to promote cyber preparedness, response, and recovery.

- The sector responded to daily cyber attacks and organized robust, sector-wide responses to major cyber threats.

Each year, the IT Sector CIKR Protection Annual Report provides updates on the sector's efforts to identify, prioritize, and coordinate the protection of its critical infrastructure. The Sector Annual Report describes the current priorities of the sector and the progress made during the past year in following the plans and strategies set out in the IT SSP.

The members of the IT SCC and the IT GCC believe that the SSP's goals, objectives, and long-term risk management plan position the sector to continue to benefit from public-private collaboration. The IT SSP identifies important opportunities for collaboration between and among the private sector, State, local, and tribal governments, nongovernmental organizations, and the Federal Government. By working together, private and public IT Sector partners can prioritize protective initiatives and investments within and across sectors. Such collaboration can ensure that limited government resources are applied effectively and efficiently. Over time, this will mitigate risks by reducing vulnerabilities, deterring threats, and minimizing the consequences of incidents. Creating a value proposition for both government and private sector participation in this process is critical to fostering increased resilience across shared IT infrastructures that enable CIKR functions.

Information Technology Sector Government Coordinating Council Letter of Concurrence

The 2010 Information Technology (IT) Sector-Specific Plan (SSP) is the result of a collaborative effort among the private sector; State, local, and tribal governments; non-governmental organizations; and the Federal Government. The 2010 IT SSP provides a strategic framework for IT Sector critical infrastructure and key resources (CIKR) protection and resilience. The combined efforts across IT Sector partnerships will result in the prioritization of protection initiatives and investments to ensure that resources can be applied where they contribute the most to risk mitigation by lowering vulnerabilities, deterring threats, and minimizing the consequences of attacks and other incidents.

During its development, the Department of Homeland Security (DHS) worked closely with members of the IT Government Coordinating Council (GCC), including representatives from the Departments of Commerce, Defense, Justice, State, and Treasury; the State, Local, Tribal, and Territorial GCC; and the National Association of State Chief Information Officers, to develop the 2010 IT SSP in partnership with the IT Sector Coordinating Council (SCC). The 2010 IT SSP details the progress the IT Sector has made in its risk management efforts, including the completion of the IT Sector Baseline Risk Assessment in 2009 and discusses how it is using the results of the assessment to inform the sector's CIKR protective programs, research and development, and measurement activities. GCC members contributed time and expertise to develop and finalize the IT SSP and will:

- Support the concepts and processes outlined in the 2010 IT SSP to carry out their assigned functional responsibilities regarding the protection of CIKR as described herein;

- Work with DHS, as appropriate and consistent with their own agency-specific authorities, resources, and programs, to implement programs that enhance CIKR protection;

- Cooperate and coordinate with DHS, in accordance with guidance provided in Homeland Security Presidential Directive 7, as appropriate and consistent with their own agency-specific authorities, resources, and programs, to facilitate CIKR protection;

- Develop or modify existing interagency and agency-specific CIKR plans, as appropriate, to incorporate concepts and actions outlined in the IT SSP;

- Maintain partnerships for CIKR protection with appropriate State, regional, local, tribal, and international entities; the private sector; and non-governmental organizations; and

- Utilize partnerships to build on the success of the IT Sector Baseline Risk Assessment to identify appropriate risk responses and mitigation strategies to reduce national-level risks.

DHS looks forward to continuing to work in partnership with IT GCC and IT SCC representatives and other sector partners on the implementation of the IT SSP.

Sincerely,

Gregory Schaffer
Assistant Secretary for Cybersecurity & Communications
U.S. Department of Homeland Security

Todd M. Keil
Assistant Secretary for Infrastructure Protection
U.S. Department of Homeland Security

October 14, 2010

The Honorable Gregory Schaffer
Assistant Secretary for Cybersecurity & Communications
U.S. Department of Homeland Security
Washington, DC 20528

Subject: Letter of Coordination, Information Technology Sector Specific Plan

Dear Assistant Secretary Schaffer:

The members of the Information Technology (IT) Sector, organized through our Sector Coordinating Council (SCC), the IT SCC, share a commitment to improving America's homeland security through our stewardship of critical technology infrastructures. We voluntarily organized to collaborate with the Department of Homeland Security (DHS) National Cyber Security Division (NCSD) and other agencies in accordance with the National Infrastructure Protection Plan to develop the updated 2010 IT Sector Specific Plan (SSP). This plan outlines national capabilities for: (1) prevention and protection through risk management; (2) situational awareness for stakeholders at all levels; (3) response, recovery, resiliency, and reconstitution of America's IT infrastructure; and (4) continuous improvement of IT Sector planning and response processes.

The plan's goals and objectives chart a course for long-term collaboration with the Federal government, especially DHS. The 2010 IT SSP identifies collaboration opportunities among the private sector, State, local, and tribal governments, nongovernmental organizations, and the Federal Government. By working together, private and public IT Sector security partners can inform the prioritization of limited government and private sector resources more effectively and efficiently.

Since the publication of the first IT SSP in 2007, the IT Sector has made significant progress in its national-level risk management efforts, including the completion of the IT Sector Baseline Risk Assessment in 2009. The 2010 IT SSP discusses how the IT Sector is using the results of that baseline analysis to inform the Sector's protective programs, research and development, and measurement activities. The IT SCC looks forward to working with its government partners on the IT SSP's long term risk management plan.

The members of the IT community, represented by the IT SCC, will continue to work collaboratively with DHS, its other government partners (federal, state, local, and tribal), and other security partners to implement the recommendations embodied in this iteration of the IT SSP.

Thank you for your continued support of the IT SCC as we focus our private and public collaboration around critical infrastructure protection. We look forward to furthering this partnership and to future engagement with other Sector Coordinating Councils and through the Partnership for Critical Infrastructure Security.

Sincerely,

Cheri F. McGuire
Chair

Ken Watson
Vice Chair

On behalf of the Membership of the IT Sector Coordinating Council

Members of the IT SCC Executive Committee:

Cheri McGuire, Symantec Corporation, Chair
Ken Watson, Cisco, Vice Chair
Brent Williams, Anakam, Secretary
Peter Allor, IBM
Guy Copeland, CSC
Larry Clinton, Internet Security Alliance
Robert Dix, Juniper Networks
Liesyl Franz, TechAmerica
Franck Journoud, Business Software Alliance
Angela McKay, Microsoft
Brian Willis, Intel Corporation (ex officio representative of the
    IT Information Sharing and Analysis Center)

IT-SCC Members:

AC Technology
Afilias USA, Inc.
Anakam Inc
Arxan Defense Systems, Inc. & Dunrath Capital
BAE Systems
BearingPoint
Bell Security Solutions
Bivio Networks
Business Software Alliance
Center for Internet Security
Certichron Inc.
Cisco Systems, Inc.
Computer and Communications Industry Association
CA Technologies
Computing Technology Industry Association
Concert Technologies
Core Security Technologies
CSC
Cyber Pack Ventures, Inc.
Dell
Deloitte & Touche LLP
Dynetics

eBay Inc.
Echelon One
EDS
EMC Corporation
Entrust, Inc.
EWA Information & Infrastructure
General Dynamics
Google
Green Hills Software
Hatha Systems
IBM
Information Sharing & Analysis Center (IT-ISAC)
Information Systems Security Association (ISSA)
Information Technology Industry Council (ITI)
Intel Corporation
International Systems Security Engineering
    Association (ISSEA)
Internet Security Alliance
ITT Corporation
Juniper Networks
KPMG
L-3 Communications

Lancope, Inc
LGS Innovations
Litmus Logic LLC
Lockheed Martin
Lumeta Corp
Lunar Line
McAfee, Inc.
Microsoft Corporation
NetStar-1, Inc.
Neustar
Northrop Grumman
NTT America
One Enterprise Consulting Group, LLC
Raytheon
Reclamere
Renesys
Research in Motion (RIM) Corp USA
SAFE-BioPharma Association
SafeNet Government Solutions
Seagate Technology
Secure Computing Corporation
SecureState, LLC
Sentar Inc.
Serco International
Siemens Healthcare, Health Services
Symantec
System 1, Inc
Team Cymru
TechAmerica
Telecontinuity, Inc.
Terremark
TestPros, Inc.
Triumfant
U.S. Internet Service Provider Association
Unisys Corporation
VeriSign
Verizon
VOSTROM Holdings Inc.

Table of Contents

List of Figures

List of Tables

Executive Summary

The 2010 Information Technology (IT) Sector-Specific Plan (SSP) represents a partnership and collaboration between the IT Sector Coordinating Council (SCC) and the Government Coordinating Council (GCC) who leverage their unique capabilities to address the complex challenges of critical infrastructure and key resources (CIKR) protection. The IT Sector entities involved in development of the 2010 SSP believe that the risk assessment and management, research and development (R&D), protective program, education and awareness, and metrics activities described in the SSP will provide value for the sector and customers who rely on its products and services. As such, IT Sector entities involved in development of the SSP will work to convey the national security and business value for participation in SSP implementation activities to other members of the IT Sector.

Sector Profile and Goals

Many CIKR sectors are primarily composed of finite and easily identifiable physical assets. Unlike such CIKR sectors, the IT Sector is a functions-based sector that comprises not only physical assets but also virtual systems and networks that enable key capabilities and services in both the public and private sectors. Six critical functions support the sector's ability to produce and provide high assurance IT products and services for various sectors. These functions are required to maintain or reconstitute networks (e.g., the Internet, local networks, and wide area networks) and their associated services. The IT Sector's six critical functions are:

- Provide IT products and services;
- Provide incident management capabilities;
- Provide domain name resolution services;
- Provide identity management and associated trust support services;
- Provide Internet-based content, information, and communications services; and,
- Provide Internet routing, access, and connection services.

These critical IT Sector functions are provided by a combination of entities—often owners and operators and their respective associations—that provide IT hardware, software, systems, and services. IT services include development, integration, operations, communications, and security.

> **IT Sector Vision**
>
> *To achieve a sustained reduction in the impact of incidents to the sector's critical functions*
>
> **Goals for the IT Sector**
>
> **Goal 1:** Identify, assess, and manage risks to the IT Sector's critical functions and international dependencies.
>
> **Goal 2:** Improve situational awareness during normal operations, potential or realized threats and disruptions, intentional or unintentional incidents, crippling attacks (cyber or physical) against IT Sector infrastructure, technological emergencies and failures, or presidentially declared disasters.
>
> **Goal 3:** Enhance the capabilities of public and private sector partners to respond to and recover from realized threats and disruptions, intentional or unintentional incidents, crippling attacks (cyber or physical) against IT Sector infrastructure, technological emergencies or failures, or presidentially declared disasters, and develop mechanisms for reconstitution.
>
> **Goal 4:** Drive continuous improvement of the IT Sector's risk management, situational awareness, and response, recovery, and reconstitution capabilities.

Functions-Based Risk Management

The IT Sector's top-down and functions-based approach assesses the sector's ability to support the economy and national security. In addition, the IT Sector's risk approach evaluates risk across the sector by focusing on critical functions rather than specific organizations or assets. This national-level perspective complements and builds on individual entities' risk management efforts.

IT Sector risk management approaches focus on two levels:

- **The individual enterprise level:** Private sector entities typically base their enterprise approaches on business objectives, such as shareholder value, efficacy, and customer service, while public sector entities usually base their enterprise approaches on ensuring mission effectiveness or providing a public service. Enterprise-level risk management approaches typically involve cybersecurity initiatives and practices to maintain the health of information security programs and infrastructures.

- **The sector or national level:** At the sector or national level, the IT Sector manages risk to its six critical functions to promote the assurance and resilience of the IT infrastructure and to protect against cascading consequences based on the sector's inter-connectedness and the critical functions' interdependencies.

IT SCC and GCC partners determined that this top-down and functions-based approach, which focuses on understanding the functions of the infrastructure rather than cataloging physical fixed assets, to be an effective approach for the highly distributed infrastructure that enables entities to produce and provide IT hardware, software, and services. The top-down approach enables public and private IT Sector partners to prioritize additional mitigations and protective measures to risks of national concern.

Risk Assessment

The IT Sector Baseline Risk Assessment (ITSRA) serves as the foundation for the sector's national-level risk management activities. Both public and private sector partners collaborated in the assessment, which reflects the expertise and the collective consensus of participating subject matter experts (SMEs). The ITSRA methodology assesses risks from manmade deliberate, manmade unintentional, and natural threats that could affect the ability of the sector's critical functions and subfunctions to support the economy and national security. The methodology leverages existing risk-related definitions, frameworks, and taxonomies from various sources, including public and private IT Sector partners, standards development organizations, and policy guidance entities. By leveraging these frameworks, the sector's methodology reflects current knowledge about risk and adapts them in a way that enables a functions-based risk assessment.

Using the threat, vulnerability, and consequence frameworks in the sector's risk assessment methodology, SMEs developed a comprehensive baseline IT Sector Risk Profile that identified risks of concern for the IT Sector. The risks of concern highlight the risks of greatest concern to the confidentiality, integrity, or availability impacts of the critical function.

Risk Response and Management

Using the risks identified in the ITSRA, the IT Sector is identifying appropriate risk responses and mitigation strategies to reduce national-level risks. Potential risk responses include improving physical security, establishing logical, electronic, or cyber access controls, or neutralizing threats before they launch. Identifying risk responses and prioritizing the mitigations for identified IT Sector risks helps ensure that resources are applied where they can most effectively respond to the threats, vulnerabilities, and consequences facing the critical IT Sector functions.

Protective Programs and Resiliency Strategies

The ITSRA illustrates the threats, vulnerabilities, and consequences facing the critical IT Sector functions. As such, the ITSRA results directly inform IT Sector risk mitigation activities (RMAs)—namely protective programs and R&D. The goal of RMA implementation is to reduce risk to the IT Sector critical functions through protective programs and R&D. As part of the National Infrastructure Protection Plan (NIPP) risk management framework, IT Sector SMEs identified key RMAs prioritized on the risks of concern identified in the ITSRA.

Measuring Effectiveness

With critical functions serving as the foundation of the IT Sector's risk management approach, the sector's measurement methodology relies on a functions-based approach to analyze the effectiveness of its efforts to mitigate CIKR risks and promote protection and resilience. Metrics enable partners to monitor the status of RMAs and facilitate improvement in the security and resilience of IT CIKR by applying corrective actions based on observed measurements.

To measure progress against the baseline ITSRA, IT Sector partners:

- Evaluate the ITSRA-identified risks, beginning with high-consequence, high-likelihood risks, across the six critical functions and the potential mitigation strategies associated with each specific risk; and

- Conduct a risk reduction activity analysis to determine if the risk should be mitigated, avoided, accepted, or transferred.

Risk reduction activity status metrics help track progress on managing the risks identified in the ITSRA. If sector partners identify risk mitigation as a response yielding the greatest potential reduction to assessed consequences, they will evaluate the estimated effect of each potential mitigation strategy to determine which strategies will result in the greatest net impact to risk reduction. IT Sector SMEs combine each mitigation activity for its relative effectiveness and feasibility rankings to arrive at an overall ranking for each potential RMA. Armed with this prioritized information, IT Sector SMEs can focus on RMAs that, through implementation of the related mitigation, provide a measurable reduction in the associated risk's likelihood, vulnerability, and consequence factors.

IT Sector SMEs then develop implementation plans for each RMA, and progress and outcome-based metrics to monitor the RMA's status and effectiveness through completion. Subsequent assessments validate these measures to determine if the RMA is indeed resulting in the forecasted risk reduction across the sector. This outcome-driven, integrated measurement approach enables the IT Sector to monitor continuously its risk posture relative to its national-level critical functions.

CIKR Protection R&D

Unlike the R&D paradigm used by the other CIKR sectors, both the government and the private sector invest significantly in cybersecurity CIKR R&D. The continuous process of innovation in the private sector fuels new products and capabilities that establish competitive differentiation among private sector entities. Leveraging private sector R&D investment while respecting the proprietary nature of some of those efforts and sharing information on government R&D initiatives and priorities are critical to the IT Sector's overall R&D strategy. To understand the challenge of collaboration better in this environment, the IT Sector partners visualize the role of public and private sector R&D as an ecosystem where the private sector focuses on certain portions of R&D that are commercially viable. R&D areas that are not private sector investment priorities represent high risk, and they should alternatively receive more investment by the Federal Government.

The IT Sector is integrating the results of the ITSRA into the IT Sector's standing working groups for action. To continue the progress achieved since the completion of the 2007 IT SSP, IT Sector partners also continue to coordinate with government agencies involved with IT R&D. The IT Sector has developed relationships with the Office of Science and Technology Policy, the Department of Homeland Security (DHS) Office of Infrastructure Protection and the Science & Technology Directorate, and the Cyber Security Information Assurance Interagency Working Group in the Networking and Information Technology Research and Development Program in anticipation of future collaboration on informing government R&D priorities. This expansion of coordination and collaboration is a vital step in recognizing the broad influence, investment, and need to coordinate with a broad constituent base to promote cyber CIKR R&D.

Managing and Coordinating Sector-Specific Agency Responsibilities

As described in Homeland Security Presidential Directive 7, DHS is responsible for managing and coordinating IT Sector CIKR protection activities, including leading the development of the SSP for the IT Sector. The Department has delegated this responsibility to the National Cyber Security Division. Sector-Specific Agency responsibilities include maintenance and update of the SSP, annual reporting, resources and budgets, and training and education.

Introduction

Homeland Security Presidential Directive 7 (HSPD-7) requires Federal agencies, coordinated by the Department of Homeland Security (DHS), to identify, prioritize, and coordinate the protection of critical infrastructure and key resources (CIKR) to prevent, deter, and mitigate the effects of efforts to destroy, incapacitate, or exploit them. Implementing this policy requires substantial commitment to public-private partnership. The directive identified 17 CIKR sectors, including the Information Technology (IT) Sector, and paired each CIKR sector with a Sector-Specific Agency (SSA) for partnering on protective initiatives.[1] HSPD-7 requires DHS to develop an overall National Infrastructure Protection Plan (NIPP), which was initially developed and published in 2006 and revised in 2009. The NIPP specifically assigns DHS the mission of establishing uniform policies, approaches, guidelines, and methodologies for integrating infrastructure protection and risk management activities within and across sectors, along with developing metrics and criteria for related programs and activities.

The NIPP and its complementary Sector-Specific Plans (SSPs) provide a consistent, unifying structure for integrating existing and future CIKR protection efforts. They also define the core processes and mechanisms for public and private sector partners to implement coordinated CIKR protection initiatives. Public and private sector partners have an enduring interest in assuring the availability of the infrastructure.

The IT Sector's market-based environment enables rapid innovation and drives investments in security to meet customers' changing needs and promote the resilience of the IT Sector. Prevention and protection through risk management, situational awareness, education, and response, recovery, and reconstitution efforts are most effective when full participation of public and private sector partners exists; such efforts suffer without the full participation of either partner.

The 2010 IT SSP represents a partnership and collaboration between the IT public and private sector entities as they leverage their unique capabilities to address the complex challenges of CIKR protection. The IT Sector entities involved in development of the 2010 SSP believe that the risk assessment and management, research and development (R&D), protective programs, education and awareness training, and metrics activities described in the SSP will provide value for the sector and customers who rely on its products and services. As such, IT Sector entities involved in development of the SSP will work to convey the national security and business value for participation in SSP implementation activities to other members of the IT Sector.

IT Sector partners, including representatives from the DHS National Cyber Security Division (NCSD), the IT Sector Coordinating Council (SCC), and the IT Government Coordinating Council (GCC), developed the 2010 IT SSP. The SSP is a planning document that focuses on meeting sector goals that are most pressing for homeland, economic, and national security purposes. The SSP does not provide specific procedures for individual IT Sector entities' operations. The SSP:

---

[1] When HSPD-7 was released, it named 17 CIKR sectors. Subsequent to its release, the Critical Manufacturing Sector was established, bringing the total number of CIKR sectors to 18.

- Establishes shared IT Sector goals and objectives and aligns initiatives to meet them;

- Describes roles, responsibilities, and opportunities that the IT SCC, IT GCC, and other partners can play in implementing the SSP;

- Outlines the IT Sector partners' risk-based approach to identify, assess, prioritize, protect, and provide opportunities for continuous improvement to critical IT Sector functions; and,

- Identifies opportunities for exercising and integrating public and private sector preparedness efforts with tools and technologies essential for effective incident response, system remediation, and reconstitution.

Document Organization

The organization of the IT SSP represents an IT SCC and GCC consensus outline based on the IT Sector's functions-based approach to risk management.

Section 1: Sector Profile and Goals. Introduces the sector's scope, partners, vision, and risk management, information-sharing, response, recovery, and continuous improvement goals.

Section 2: Functions-Based Risk Management. Discusses the sector's top-down, functions-based approach to risk management and introduces the sector's risk assessment methodology.

Section 3: Risk Assessment. Explains the sector's risk assessment methodology, including threat, vulnerability, and consequence assessments.

Section 4: Risk Response and Management Efforts. Illustrates the sector's approach to risk-based mitigation prioritization across the six critical functions based on vulnerability and feasibility factors.

Section 5: Protective Programs and Resiliency Strategies. Provides an overall view of the sector's approach to protective program identification and prioritization.

Section 6: Measure Effectiveness. Explains the sector's risk mitigation activity (RMA) measurement approach and the use of progress, status, and outcome measures to promote continuous improvement.

Section 7: CIKR Protection R&D. Provides an overview of the sector's approach to R&D requirements, identification, and implementation.

Section 8: Managing and Coordinating SSA Responsibilities. Discusses SSA management and coordination of management and processes with IT Sector and other CIKR partners.

1. Sector Profile and Goals

1.1 Sector Profile

1.1.1 Definition

The Homeland Security Act of 2002 required the first-ever all-encompassing coordinated national CIKR protection effort. HSPD-7 identifies 17 CIKR sectors, including the IT Sector, and requires Federal agencies, coordinated by DHS, to identify, prioritize, and coordinate the protection of the Nation's CIKR.[2] The NIPP and its complementary SSPs provide a consistent, unifying structure for integrating existing and future CIKR protection efforts. They also provide the core processes and mechanisms to enable government and private sector partners to work together to implement CIKR protection initiatives.[3]

Many CIKR sectors are primarily composed of finite and easily identifiable physical assets. Unlike such CIKR sectors, the IT Sector is a functions-based sector that comprises not only physical assets but also virtual systems and networks that enable key capabilities and services in both public and private sectors. Functions are sets of processes that produce, provide, and maintain products and services. These functions encompass the full set of processes involved in creating IT products and services, including R&D, manufacturing, distribution, upgrades, and maintenance. They also support the sector's ability to produce and provide high-assurance products, services, and practices that are resilient to threats and can be rapidly recovered. Assurance is essential to achieving the sector's vision and is therefore a fundamental aspect of all critical functions. The functions are not limited by geographic or political boundaries, further defining its virtual and distributed nature. This highlights the increasing need for international collaboration and coordination for risk assessment activities, effective security practices, and protective program design and implementation.

Six critical functions support the sector's ability to produce and provide high assurance IT products and services for various sectors. These functions are required to maintain or reconstitute networks (e.g., the Internet, local networks, and wide area networks) and their associated services. Figure 1-1 presents the IT SCC and GCC consensus on critical functions that are vital to national and economic security and public health, safety, and confidence. These functions are distributed across a broad network of infrastructure, managed proactively, and therefore, can withstand and rapidly recover from most threats.[4]

---

[2] When HDPD-7 was released, it named 17 CIKR sectors. Subsequent to its release, the Critical Manufacturing Sector was establishing, bringing the total number of CIKR sectors to 18.

[3] For more information on the NIPP, please see the following Web site: **http://www.dhs.gov/files/programs/editorial_0827.shtm.**

[4] For additional information on the capability of IT Sector functions to withstand and rapidly recover from most threats, please see the IT Sector Baseline Risk Assessment: **http://www.it-scc.org/documents/itscc/IT_Sector_Risk_Assessment_Report_Final.pdf.**

Figure 1-1: IT Sector Critical Functions

IT Sector Function	Description
Provide IT Products and Services	The IT Sector conducts operations and services that provide for the design, development, distribution, and support of IT products (hardware and software) and operational support services that are essential or critical to the assurance of national and economic security and public health, safety, and confidence. These hardware and software products and services are limited to those necessary to maintain or reconstitute the network and its associated services.
Provide Incident Management Capabilities	The IT Sector develops, provides, and operates incident management capabilities for itself and other sectors that are essential or critical to the assurance of national and economic security and public health, safety, and confidence.
Provide Domain Name Resolution Services	The IT Sector provides and operates domain registration services, top-level domain (TLD)/root infrastructures, and resolution services that are essential or critical to the assurance of national and economic security and public health, safety, and confidence.
Provide Identity Management and Associated Trust Support Services	The IT Sector produces and provides technologies, services, and infrastructure to ensure the identity of, authenticate, and authorize entities and ensure confidentiality, integrity, and availability of devices, services, data, and transactions that are essential or critical to the assurance of national and economic security and public health, safety, and confidence.
Provide Internet-based Content, Information, and Communications Services	The IT Sector produces and provides technologies, services, and infrastructure that deliver key content, information, and communications capabilities that are essential or critical to the assurance of national and economic security and public health, safety, and confidence.
Provide Internet Routing, Access, and Connection Services	The IT Sector (in close collaboration with the Communications Sector) provides and supports Internet backbone infrastructures, points of presence, peering points, local access services, and capabilities that are essential or critical to the assurance of national and economic security and public health, safety, and confidence.

These critical IT Sector functions are provided by a combination of entities—often owners and operators and their respective associations—who provide IT hardware, software, systems, and services. IT services include development, integration, operations, communications, and security.

1.1.2 Scope

In August 2009, the IT Sector released its IT Sector Baseline Risk Assessment (ITSRA). The results of the ITSRA inform the IT SSP and other IT Sector plans, reports, and initiatives to:

- Ensure the security, resilience, and reliability of the Nation's IT and communications infrastructure; and,

- Prevent, protect against, mitigate, and prepare for nationally significant events; technological emergencies; or presidentially declared disasters that threaten, disrupt, or cripple IT Sector functions.

Specifically, the IT SSP is concerned with all-hazard events that have cyber or physical consequences which:[5]

---

[5] The 2009 NIPP defines the term *all-hazard* as follows: A grouping classification encompassing all conditions, environmental or manmade, that have the potential to cause injury, illness, or death; damage to or loss of equipment, infrastructure services, or property; or alternatively causing functional degradation to social, economic, or environmental aspects.

- Cause, or are likely to cause, harm to mission-critical functions by negatively impacting the confidentiality, integrity, or availability of electronic information, information systems, services, or networks; or

- Threaten public health or safety, undermine public confidence, have a negative effect on the national economy, or diminish the security posture of the Nation.

1.2 Critical Infrastructure and Key Resources Partners

The NIPP describes a sector partnership model that encourages the public and private sectors to collaborate on their respective infrastructure protection activities. This collaboration is accomplished through SCCs—comprising industry and private sector partners—and GCCs—comprising Federal, State, local, tribal, and territorial government entities.

The IT SCC and GCC are the primary bodies for communicating their respective perspectives and developing collaborative policies, strategies, and security efforts to advance critical infrastructure protection.

1.2.1 IT GCC Membership

The IT GCC comprises Federal, State, and local governments as providers of IT services that meet the needs of citizens, businesses, and employees. Table 1-1 lists the IT GCC members.

Table 1-1: IT GCC Membership

IT GCC Membership	

· Department of Commerce
  – National Institute of Standards and Technology
· Department of Defense
· Department of Energy
· Department of Homeland Security
  – National Protection and Programs Directorate (NPPD)
    » National Cyber Security Division (NCSD) – IT GCC Chair
    » Office of Infrastructure Protection
    » National Communications System (NCS)
    » Office of Emergency Communications (OEC)
  – Science and Technology Directorate
  – Office of Intelligence and Analysis
  – Transportation Security Administration
	· Department of the Interior
	· Department of Justice
	· Department of State
	· Department of the Treasury
	· General Services Administration
	· National Association of State Chief Information Officers
	· State, Local, Tribal, and Territorial Government Coordinating Council

1.2.2 IT SCC Membership

IT SCC members, listed in table 1-2, include the following types of private sector entities:[6]

- Domain Name System (DNS) root and Generic Top-Level Domain (gTLD) operators;

- Internet service providers (ISPs);

- Internet backbone providers;

---

[6] IT Sector partner categories are adapted from the *Bylaws of Information Technology Sector Coordinating Council*, January 2007.

- Internet portal and e-mail providers;

- Networking hardware companies (e.g., systems manufacturers producing router, firewall, security appliance, wide area network (WAN) accelerators, application gateways, other comprehensive platforms, fiber-optics makers and line acceleration hardware manufacturers) and other hardware manufacturers (e.g., personal computers, servers, and information storage);

- Network Security Information Exchange (NSIE);

- Software companies;

- Security services vendors;

- Communications companies that characterize themselves as having an IT role;

- Edge and core service providers;

- IT system integrators; and

- IT security associations.

Table 1-2: IT SCC Membership[7]

IT SCC Membership		
• AC Technology, Inc.	• General Atomics	• Neustar
• Afilias USA, Inc.	• General Dynamics	• Northrop Grumman
• Anakam, Inc.	• Google	• NTT America
• Arxan Defense Systems, Inc. & Dunrath Capital	• Green Hills Software	• One Enterprise Consulting Group, LLC
• Bell Security Solutions Inc.	• Hatha Systems	• Perot Systems
• Business Software Alliance	• IBM Corporation	• R & H Security Consulting LLC
• Center for Internet Security	• Information Systems Security Association (ISSA)	• Raytheon
• Cisco Systems, Inc.		• Reclamere
• Computer and Communications Industry Association	• Intel Corporation	• Renesys Corporation
	• Information Technology - Information Sharing & Analysis Center (IT-ISAC)	• Seagate Technology
• Computer Associates International		• Sentar Inc
• Computer Sciences Corporation	• International Systems Security Engineering Association (ISSEA)	• Siemens Healthcare
• Core Security Technologies		• SI International
• Cyber Pack Ventures Inc.	• Internet Security Alliance	• Sun Microsystems, Inc
• Cyber Security Industry Alliance	• IBM Internet Security Systems, Inc.	• Symantec Corporation
• Computing Technology Industry Association	• International Security Trust and Privacy Alliance	• System 1
	• ITT Corporation	• TechAmerica
• Concert Technologies	• Juniper Networks	• Telecontinuity, Inc.
• Deloitte & Touche LLP	• KPMG LLP	• Terremark World Wide
• Detica	• L-3 Communications	• TestPros, Inc.
• Ebay	• Lancope, Inc	• Triumfant
• EDS	• Litmus Logic	• U.S. Internet Service Provider Association
• Electronic Industries Alliance	• LGS Innovations	
• EMC Corporation	• Lockheed Martin	• Unisys Corporation
• Entrust, Inc.	• Lumeta Corporation	• VeriSign
• EWA Information & Infrastructure Technologies, Inc.	• McAfee, Inc.	• Verizon
	• Microsoft Corporation	• VOSTROM

---

[7] Current as of July 2009.

1.2.3 IT Sector Information Sharing

Effective information sharing enables the success of the IT Sector's public-private partnership model by ensuring that all partners have relevant situational awareness to protect IT CIKR and critical functions. Each stakeholder—Intelligence Community (IC) members; Law Enforcement (LE) agencies; CIKR owners and operators; and information-sharing and analysis organizations—possesses unique information that other partners may need. Timely dissemination of sensitive and actionable information allows recipients to take appropriate actions; however, recipients of that information must protect it from disclosure to entities that might use it to the detriment of originators or recipients. This complex, multifaceted information-sharing architecture enables all other sector functions, including risk assessment, implementation of protective programs, collection and sharing of metrics, collaborative R&D, and response to and recovery from exceptional events.

1.2.3.1 Policy Information Sharing

IT Sector partners are active participants in cross-sector security policy forums, including the Partnership for Critical Infrastructure Security (PCIS), the Cross-Sector Cyber Security Working Group (CSCSWG), the Network Security Information Exchanges, and the Industrial Control System Joint Working Group (ICSJWG).

PCIS and the CIKR Cross-Sector Council focus primarily on cross-sector policy, strategy, and interdependency issues affecting the critical infrastructure sectors. Membership includes the leadership from each of the SCCs, including the IT SCC, which represents the owners and operators of the CIKR sectors.

The CSCSWG was established to improve cross-sector cybersecurity protection efforts across the Nation's CIKR sectors by identifying opportunities to improve sector coordination around cybersecurity issues and topics, highlighting cyber dependencies and interdependencies, and sharing government and private sector cybersecurity products and findings. The working group serves as a forum for public and private sector partners to share perspectives, knowledge, and subject matter expertise on a wide range of cybersecurity issues. The CSCSWG aligns with the NIPP sector partnership model, and thus includes members from the SCCs and GCCs of the 18 CIKR sectors.

The IT Sector provides leadership to the CSCSWG's vital cybersecurity mission by prioritizing topics for discussion and supporting targeted cybersecurity activities in the CSCSWG. Under the auspices of the CSCSWG, the IT Sector has supported two targeted activities as part of the Comprehensive National Cybersecurity Initiative (CNCI): the Incentives Subgroup and the Metrics Subgroup.

- **The Incentives Subgroup** developed cybersecurity incentive recommendations, across all CIKR sectors, to drive improvement in the private sector's cybersecurity posture, such as incentives for voluntary vulnerability assessments, where market forces alone yield an insufficient value proposition.

- **The Metrics Subgroup** works with participating CIKR sectors to identify sector cybersecurity metrics to promote continuous cybersecurity improvement across the CIKR sectors.

In 1991, the National Communications System (NCS) and the National Security Telecommunications Advisory Committee (NSTAC) established Government and NSTAC Network Security Information Exchanges (NSIE), respectively, to exchange information in the industry and between the government and industry on electronic intrusion threats to the Public Network (PN) and its vulnerabilities. The objective of the NSIE is to improve the overall security of the computers and associated databases in the PN. Participating NSIE organizations exchange information during meetings, which are held every two months, and between meetings through the US-Computer Emergency Readiness Team (US-CERT) portal.

IT Sector partners also participate in cross-sector efforts to secure control systems. The DHS Control Systems Security Program (CSSP) established the ICSJWG to facilitate information sharing and reduce the risk to the Nation's industrial control systems. Industrial control systems (ICS) (also known as Supervisory Control and Data Acquisition (SCADA)) systems, process control systems (PCS), and distributed control systems (DCS) are essential to industry and government alike because these systems support the operation of our Nation's CIKR. To reflect this, the goal of ICSJWG is to enhance the collaborative efforts of the ICS stakeholder community in securing CIKR by accelerating the design, development, and deployment of secure industrial control systems.

ICSJWG is a collaborative and coordinating body operating under Critical Infrastructure Partnership Advisory Council (CIPAC) requirements that provides a vehicle for communicating and partnering across all CIKR between Federal agencies and departments, as well as private asset owners and operators of ICS. The NCSD CSSP serves as the government lead in ICSJWG and is complemented by representation from a broad spectrum of IT and other CIKR sector partners.

1.2.3.2 Operational Information Sharing

In additional to sharing security policy information, the IT Sector also actively conducts operational information sharing. US-CERT is the IT Sector's public sector focal point for coordinating the sharing and analysis of operational and strategic information between and among IT Sector partners; other CIKR sectors; Federal, State, and local governments; international entities; and academic institutions. Consistent with the NIPP partnership model and fully endorsed by the IT SCC, the Information Technology-Information Sharing and Analysis Center (IT-ISAC) is the primary operational information-sharing entity for the private sector. IT-ISAC collaborates with US-CERT and the Multi State ISAC (MS-ISAC) to promote bidirectional information sharing and situational awareness.

From a control systems perspective, the CSSP also supports the Industrial Control Systems Cyber Emergency Response Team (ICS-CERT), in coordination with US-CERT for control systems-related incidents and cybersecurity situational awareness activities, and ICS-CERT maintains a technical support center to assess commercially available control systems and components.

1.2.4 Department of Homeland Security

The DHS Office of Cybersecurity and Communications (CS&C), in collaboration with public and private sector partners, works to ensure the security, resilience, and reliability of the Nation's cyber and communications infrastructure. The office comprises NCSD, NCS, and OEC, and oversees US-CERT, NCSD's operational arm. DHS is designated as the IT SSA.[8] This responsibility is delegated to NCSD, which coordinates with other government departments and agencies (through the IT GCC) and the private sector (through the IT SCC) to develop and implement the IT SSP.

IT Sector partners coordinate with DHS to promote response and recovery throughout the IT Sector. The IT-ISAC and US-CERT maintain ongoing communications. During cyber incidents, the National Cybersecurity and Communications Integration Center (NCCIC) enables representatives from the IT and Communications Sectors and ISACs to share information and coordinate response strategies in real time. Similarly, during physical security incidents, the primary means the IT Sector uses to conduct incident coordination with DHS is through communications between dedicated IT Sector liaisons and the National Incident Coordinating Center (NICC).

1.2.5 Other Federal Departments and Agencies

The responsibilities of other Federal departments and agencies are different from the SSA responsibilities. For example, under the Federal Information Security Management Act, the Office of Management and Budget (OMB) and the National Institute of Standards Technology (NIST) have responsibility for overseeing the security of the Federal Government's IT assets, systems, networks, and functions and providing guidance. Federal law enforcement agencies, such as the Federal Bureau of Investigation (FBI), play a critical role in investigating threats and prosecuting the perpetrators of cyber and physical crimes. The IC uses national-level intelligence capabilities and resources to identify and counter threats. LE and the IC provide early warning

---

[8] 2009 National Infrastructure Protection Plan.

or potential target information that can help the IT Sector and homeland security community implement preventive and protective measures.

1.2.6 State, Local, Tribal, and Territorial Governments

State and local governments provide IT services that fulfill the needs of their citizens, businesses, and employees. The National Association of State Chief Information Officers (NASCIO), which represents senior IT leaders in each State, is a key partner of the IT Sector. The MS-ISAC is a collaborative organization with participation from all 50 States, the District of Columbia, local governments, and U.S. Territories, with the mission of providing a common mechanism for raising the level of cybersecurity readiness and response for all participants. State governments engage in IT Sector activities through NASCIO's participation in the IT GCC. Local governments engage in IT Sector activities through the State, Local, Tribal, and Territorial Government Coordinating Council (SLTTGCC) participation in the IT GCC.

1.2.7 International Organizations and Foreign Partners

Because the IT Sector is global, interconnected, and interdependent, international partners play a key role in the prevention, protection, response, and recovery of critical IT Sector functions. Establishing and maintaining consistent and reliable relationships with international partners is vital to ensuring the security of the sector.

The IT Sector enjoys multiple memberships in the global Forum of Incident Response and Security Teams (FIRST), which brings together various computer security incident response teams from government, commercial, and educational organizations to enable incident response teams to respond both reactively and proactively to security incidents. In addition to FIRST, many IT Sector members participate in the Network Service Provider Security forum (NSP-SEC), a volunteer incident response mailing list, which coordinates the interaction between ISPs and Network Service Providers (NSPs) in near real time, tracks exploits and compromised systems, and mitigates the effects of exploits on ISP networks. IT Sector members are also involved in operating Internet Protocol (IP) networks belong to the North American Network Operators' Group (NANOG), a forum for coordination and dissemination of technical information on the network backbone and operations. IT Sector partners involved in IP network operations also participate in the American Registry for Internet Numbers (ARIN), the organization that manages IP allocation for the United States, Mexico, Canada, and the Caribbean. Many IT Sector partners also participate in the Internet Governance Forum (IGF), a multi-stakeholder dialog on public policy related to Internet governance issues convened under the auspices of the United Nations. The IT Sector is also well represented at meetings of the Internet Corporation for Assigned Names and Numbers (ICANN), a nonprofit organization that coordinates the domain name and addressing system. Finally, many IT Sector partners participate in the Internet Engineering Task Force (IETF), the international organization that develops Internet standards and protocols.

Tabletop, regional, national-level, and international cyber exercises provide an opportunity for sector partners to plan and test cybersecurity policies and response and recovery actions with international partners. For example, in addition to Federal, State, local, and private sector participants, Cyber Storm II featured international participation from Australia, Canada, New Zealand, and the United Kingdom.

The IT Sector also participates in the DHS Critical Foreign Dependencies Initiative (CFDI), which extends the sector's protection strategy overseas to include important foreign infrastructure that, if attacked or destroyed, could critically impact the United States. Along the same lines as CFDI, DHS/NCSD participates with the Department of State in an inter-agency international critical infrastructure protection working group to prioritize international critical infrastructure protection (CIP) efforts.

DHS/NCSD, as the IT SSA, engages in key international relationship building and information-sharing efforts to address the global nature of cybersecurity. NCSD participates in regional, bilateral, and multilateral relationships and forums that improve incident response capabilities, contribute to global cybersecurity capacity-building efforts, and coordinate on strategic policy issues. These efforts involve serving as the DHS international cybersecurity point of contact, meeting with foreign government counterparts to discuss policy and operational issues, and creating and facilitating opportunities for DHS engagement in international activities.

The NCSD Outreach and Awareness (O&A) Program conducts international outreach and facilitates collaboration, cooperation, planning, and policy development on global cybersecurity issues. Specifically, NCSD O&A collaborates with key international partners, listed in table 1-3, to manage global cyber risk through enhanced information sharing and situational awareness, improved incident response capabilities, and coordination on strategic policy issues.

Table 1-3: DHS NCSD International Program Involvement

International Programs	
International Watch and Warning Network (IWWN)	IWWN is a forum of 15 countries (Australia, Canada, Finland, France, Germany, Hungary, Japan, Italy, the Netherlands, New Zealand, Norway, Sweden, Switzerland, the United Kingdom (U.K.), and the United States) with the goal to facilitate member country cooperation and coordination on cybersecurity information sharing and incident response.
The Usual Five (U5)	The U5 is a partnership among Australia, Canada, New Zealand, the U.K., and the United States whose mission is to collaborate on cybersecurity matters.
The Group of 8 (G8)	In the G8, the Lyon-Roma High-Tech Crimes Subgroup (HTCSG) is led by the Department of Justice and is the only Lyon-Roma subgroup chaired by the United States. Working with DHS and other government agencies, HTCSG focuses on critical information infrastructure protection (CIIP) issues, usually from a law enforcement perspective.
Meridian	The Meridian Process and Conference fosters government-to-government information sharing on cybersecurity with the global community and seeks to build trust and relationships, share information, and advance government-to-government cooperation and collaboration.
The Internet Engineering Task Force	The IETF is a large, open international community of network designers, operators, vendors, and researchers concerned with the evolution of Internet architecture and the smooth operation of the Internet.
International Telecommunications Union (ITU)	The ITU is a United Nations-sponsored organization of 191 member countries and 700 nongovernment organizations. ITU provides an opportunity to engage with nations that are typically not represented in other forums, such as African and Southwest Asian nations.
Asian-Pacific Economic Cooperation (APEC)	APEC is a multilateral forum of 21 member economies that promotes cooperation on economic and select security topics in the Asia-Pacific region. NCSD provides a leadership role for the U.S. Government, serving as Deputy Convener of the Security and Prosperity Steering Group.
Organization for Economic Cooperation and Development (OECD)	OECD is a multilateral organization of 30 member countries that develops policy to sustain information security and privacy in the global networked society.
Bilateral Engagements	Bilateral engagements provide opportunities for formal and informal diplomatic relations government-to-government to discuss areas of mutual concern, build partnerships, and provide important insight into domestic activities of countries of interest.
Forum of Incident Response and Security Teams	FIRST is the premier organization and recognized global leader in incident response. Membership in FIRST enables incident response teams to respond effectively to security incidents reactive as well as proactive.

1.3 Sector Goals and Objectives

Public and private sector partners collaborated to identify overarching sector goals that support efforts to prevent, prepare for, protect against, mitigate, respond to, and recover from nationally significant events, technological emergencies, or presidentially declared disasters that threaten, disrupt, or cripple IT Sector functions. These goals create a mutually beneficial framework to develop risk management and protective strategies that will enhance sector security. Pursuit of these goals requires action by a wide array of public and private partners, including the commitment of expertise and the identification and prioritization of resources. IT Sector partners review these goals and progress toward implementing them annually. The goals and their associated objectives are listed in table 1-4.

1.3.1 Vision Statement

The IT Sector provides an infrastructure upon which all other CIKR sectors rely. As such, the IT Sector's vision is to achieve a sustained reduction in the impact of incidents on the sector's critical functions. This vision supports:

- The Federal Government's performance of essential national security missions and preservation of general public health and safety;
- State and local governments' abilities to maintain order and deliver minimum essential public services; and
- The orderly functioning of the economy.

1.3.2 Goals & Objectives

Table 1-4: IT Sector Goals and Objectives

Sector Goals	
Goal 1: Prevention and Protection through Risk Management	Identify, assess, and manage risks to the IT Sector's critical functions and international dependencies.
Objective 1.1	Periodically validate critical IT Sector functions that support the Nation's security, economy, public health, and safety.
Objective 1.2	Use the results of the baseline IT Sector Risk Assessment to identify and prioritize protective programs and R&D priorities to mitigate IT Sector risks.
Objective 1.3	Encourage IT Sector and international entities to exchange information about risk management strategies, dependencies, and interdependencies to foster a better understanding of how they improve the overall posture of the sector.
Goal 2: Enhance Situational Awareness for Stakeholders at all Appropriate Levels	Improve situational awareness during normal operations, potential or realized threats and disruptions, intentional or unintentional incidents, crippling attacks (cyber or physical) against IT Sector infrastructure, technological emergencies or failures, or presidentially declared disasters.
Objective 2.1	Define IT Sector partner information-sharing needs and routinely collaborate, develop, and disseminate targeted threat and vulnerability information at the lowest level of classification possible to ensure appropriate distribution.

Sector Goals	
Objective 2.2	Expand strategic analytical capabilities that facilitate public and private sector partner collaboration to identify potential incidents.
Objective 2.3	Facilitate integration and information sharing among the IT SCC, the IT-ISAC, and the National Cybersecurity & Communications Integration Center in Fiscal Year 2010.
Goal 3: Response, Recovery, and Reconstitution	Enhance the capabilities of public and private sector partners to respond to and recover from realized threats and disruptions, intentional or unintentional incidents, crippling attacks (cyber or physical) against IT Sector infrastructure, technological emergencies or failures, or presidentially declared disasters, and develop mechanisms for reconstitution.
Objective 3.1	Develop and maintain incident response and coordination plans and procedures, and exercise them periodically to ensure readiness and resilience.
Objective 3.2	Leverage existing or establish new mechanisms and processes for communicating with other sectors during contingencies and conduct periodic tests of the resulting communications plans and programs.
Goal 4: Continuous Improvement	Drive continuous improvement of the IT Sector's risk management, situational awareness, and response, recovery, and reconstitution capabilities.
Objective 4.1	Update the IT Sector Risk Assessment methodology based on previous results and lessons learned and use the updated methodology to periodically assess risk across the sector's critical functions.
Objective 4.2	Develop and implement exercises to validate the sector's ability to share targeted threat and vulnerability data.
Objective 4.3	Develop and implement exercises to test the sector's response, recovery, and reconstitution capabilities, to include out-of-band communications and data delivery.
Objective 4.4	Develop an incident impact taxonomy to facilitate measurement of the impact of incidents on sector critical functions.

1.4 Value Proposition

The IT Sector public-private partnership model enables partners to collaboratively identify threats and vulnerabilities to IT Sector critical functions and exchange mitigating and preventive tactics and resources to address them. Through continued public-private sector information sharing and enhanced cross-sector engagement, the IT Sector will be better prepared to:

• Shape CIP cybersecurity policy;

• Enhance the security and resilience of the critical IT Sector functions;

• Identify specific information each sector partner wants to share, who needs it, and why and how to protect it;

• Improve public-private problem solving by deepening understanding of government and industry sector security requirements;

• Share and apply effective industry security practices; and

• Assist in planning and developing DHS National Level Exercises to promote expeditious incident response capabilities.

2. Functions-Based Risk Management

The IT Sector manages global operations that are interdependent and connected with other infrastructures, many of which are international. These operations daily face numerous multifaceted global threats from natural and manmade events. Many of these events occur frequently, but do not have significant consequences because of individual entities' existing security and response capabilities. Some of these threats, however, are strategic and could affect critical functions and other elements of the Nation's critical infrastructure. The high degree of the IT Sector's interdependency, interconnectedness, and anonymity of actors makes identifying threats, assessing vulnerabilities, and estimating consequence at the national level difficult. For that reason, the sector uses a collaborative and iterative risk management approach.

2.1 Developing an IT Sector Risk Management Approach

A national-level understanding of cyber and physical risks informs risk assessment practices and resource allocation for risk mitigation by both public and private sector partners. The IT Sector's top-down and functions-based approach considers the sector's ability to support the economy and national security. In addition, the IT Sector's risk approach evaluates risk across the sector by focusing on critical functions rather than specific organizations or assets. This national-level perspective complements and builds on individual entities' risk management efforts. Figure 2-1 summarizes the methodology developed by IT Sector partners to develop a baseline IT Sector risk profile.

2.1.1 IT Sector Risk Environment

Threats to the IT Sector are complex and varied. In addition to the risks presented by manmade unintentional and natural threats, the IT Sector also faces cyber and physical threats from criminals, hackers, terrorists, and nation-states, all of whom have demonstrated a varying degree of capabilities and intentions to attack critical IT Sector functions. Manmade threats have also rapidly evolved from physical sabotage to simple automated worms and viruses to complex social engineering attacks that exploit known and unknown vulnerabilities in IT products and services.

Figure 2-1: IT Sector Risk Assessment Methodology

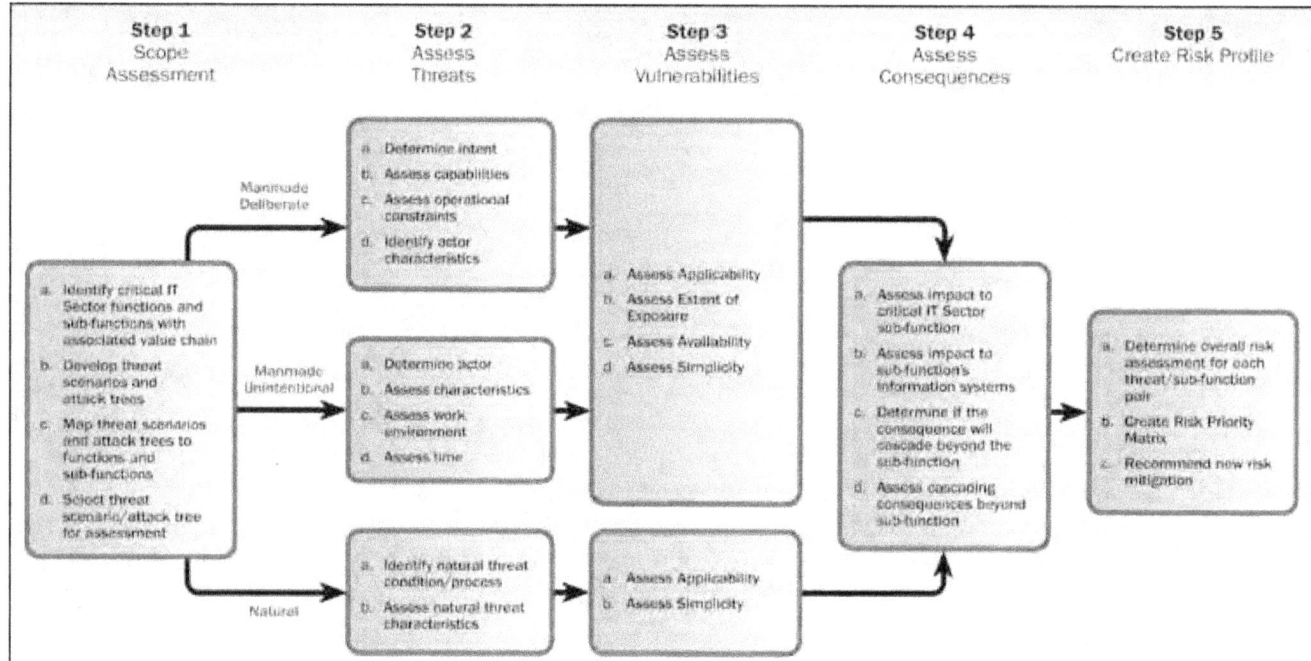

2.1.2 Risk Management Approaches in the IT Sector

IT Sector risk management approaches focus on two levels: (1) the individual enterprise level and (2) the sector or national level. Private sector entities typically base their enterprise approaches on business objectives, such as shareholder value, efficacy, and customer service. Public sector entities usually base their enterprise approaches on ensuring mission effectiveness or providing a public service. Enterprise-level risk management approaches typically involve cybersecurity initiatives and practices to maintain the health of information security programs and infrastructures. Examples of these actions include physical vulnerability mitigation measures (e.g., physical access control and surveillance); human vulnerability mitigation measures (e.g., employee screening and security training and awareness); cybersecurity measures (e.g., encryption; behavior monitoring and management technologies; independent third-party security posture assessments); and business continuity planning. These individual risk management efforts are designed to support organizational objectives and—in aggregate—they enhance the security and resilience of the IT Sector.

2.1.3 Sector or National-level IT Sector Risk Management Approach

At the sector or national-level, the IT Sector manages risk to its six critical functions to promote the assurance and resilience of the IT infrastructure and to protect against cascading consequences based on the sector's interconnectedness and the critical functions' interdependencies. IT SCC and GCC partners determined that this top-down and functions-based approach, which focuses on understanding the functions of the infrastructure rather than cataloging physical fixed assets, to be an effective approach for the highly distributed infrastructure that enables entities to produce and provide IT hardware, software, and services. The top-down approach enables public and private IT Sector partners to prioritize additional mitigation and protective measures to risks of national concern.

The purpose of using a top-down approach to assessing functions is to identify those functions that meet a minimum consequence threshold primarily based on resilience. Resources can then be devoted to analyzing nationally consequential functions and their supporting infrastructure.

2.2 Identifying Functions

The criticality of the IT Sector functions is based on their potential impact on government or sector missions, independent of any specific threat. A function's criticality depends on many factors, such as tolerable magnitude and duration of loss or degradation of the particular function. The resilience of functions to disruption or degradation increases with the availability of substitutes for the products and services, resulting from a given critical function with the degree of diversity that exists in the functions' processes and with diversity of providers. A disruption or degradation of a function can have a cascading effect, if other functions are highly dependent on its outputs.

The six IT Sector critical functions have been screened and prioritized based on HSPD-7 consequence categories and criteria for evaluating nationally significant events. The IT Sector's consequence framework provides insight to the threshold or additional factors considered when assessing overall risk to the critical functions. The evaluation criteria are:

- **Governance Impact:** Effects on Federal, State, and local governments;

- **Economic Security Impact:** Effects on users and greater economy;

- **Public Health and Safety Impact:** Effects on human health by injuries and loss of life; and

- **Public Confidence Impact:** Effects on the public's morale caused by real or perceived impacts to the critical IT Sector functions (these effects can result from the visibility of the impact, the number of people affected, and the length of time needed to switch to alternative sources).

3. Risk Assessment

3.1 Developing a Sector Risk Profile

The IT Sector Baseline Risk Assessment (ITSRA) serves as the foundation for the sector's national-level risk management activities. Both public and private sector partners collaborated in the assessment, which reflects the expertise and collective consensus of participating SMEs.

The IT Sector-wide risk approach is not intended to conflict with individual company, organizational, or enterprise risk management activities. ITSRA is intended to provide a sector and national level all-hazards risk profile that includes natural and manmade physical and cybersecurity risks; encourage informed resource allocation for IT Sector protection and management of its inherent risks; and increase awareness of risk across public and private sectors.

The assessment addresses those operational or strategic risks to the IT Sector infrastructure that are of national concern, based on the knowledge and subject matter expertise of participants in the sector's risk assessment activities. The assessment does not address all threat scenarios faced by IT Sector entities or their users and customers. As noted in specific sections of the assessment, some areas require additional collaborative study and further review. ITSRA also presents potential mitigation strategies for implementation; they are not intended to name or mandate the establishment or enhancement of specific public or private sector programs.

IT Sector Baseline Risk Assessment Development

After refining the IT Sector risk assessment methodology (see figure 2-1), the IT Sector conducted a pilot risk assessment in March 2008 to validate the accuracy and usability of the IT Sector risk methodology and test the assessment process. The lessons learned from the pilot risk assessment were incorporated in the IT Sector risk methodology through an iterative process.

The baseline ITSRA, which was conducted from September 2008 through August 2009, consisted of three phases: (1) attack tree development; (2) risk evaluation; and (3) analysis and reporting.

The IT Sector Baseline Risk Assessment report was released to the public in August 2009.

3.2 Assessing IT Sector Risk

The ITSRA methodology assesses risks from manmade deliberate, manmade unintentional, and natural threats that could affect the ability of the sector's critical functions and subfunctions to support the economy and national security. The methodology leverages existing risk-related definitions, frameworks, and taxonomies from various entities, including public and private IT Sector partners and standards and guidance organizations. By leveraging these frameworks, the sector's methodology reflects current knowledge about risk and adapts them in a way that enables a functions-based risk assessment. Results from the ITSRA will be used to inform protective programs and R&D activities to manage overall sector risk.

IT Sector Baseline Risk Assessment Impact

The result of the ITSRA is a sector-wide risk profile that describes the sector-wide risks as well as the function-specific risks and their associated existing mitigations.

This profile can be used to develop the risk management strategy for each of the functions and guide mitigation decisions. Doing so will make efficient use of resources that are needed for mitigation steps and take measures that will reduce, avoid, or eliminate risks in the future.

3.2.1 Assessing Threats

The threat analysis approach considers the full spectrum of intentional and unintentional manmade and natural threats. Because of the different intrinsic qualities of manmade deliberate, manmade unintentional, and natural threats, the risk assessment methodology includes unique, but comparable, components for analyzing these threats and their associated vulnerabilities. These factors flow into a common consequence evaluation for all threats to the critical functions.

Traditional threat analysis generally identifies an actor and the actor's intentions, motives, and capabilities to compromise a given target. Such approaches typically rely on historical data associated with a particular actor to predict threats. When analyzing threats to the IT Sector, this traditional approach to threat assessment alone is not sufficient in the sector's risk environment because actors are not easily identifiable or traceable, and attacks—deliberate or unintentional—can go from conception to exploitation in hours. The IT Sector's approach, illustrated in figure 3-1, complements the traditional threat assessment approach because it addresses capability and intent factors independent of known actors and considers emerging nontraditional threats.

The IT Sector's threat assessment approach is designed to identify threats that have national significance based on capabilities. This approach is consistent with traditional threat analysis approaches, which typically focus on specific actors and evaluate their capabilities. Because of the difficulty with identifying threat actors, especially in cyberspace, the IT Sector focuses on a threat's capabilities to exploit vulnerabilities before identifying specific actors.

The sector defines threat capability as the availability or the ease of use of tools or methods that could be used to damage, disrupt, or destroy critical functions. For natural threat, capability is inherent; therefore, the assessment considers natural threats that could have a nationally significant impact. A capabilities-based approach is applied differently for intentional manmade threats. For intentional manmade threats, widely available tools or methods that can be easily configured to exploit critical functions present significant challenges. The IT Sector is also vulnerable to unintentional manmade threat because of its high reliance on human interaction and skill sets.

Threat Categories

The **manmade deliberate threat** component focuses on incidents that are either enabled or deliberately caused by human beings with malicious intent. It facilitates a qualitative assessment of these threats by analyzing their intent and capabilities and identifying the actors' characteristics.

The **manmade unintentional threat** component focuses on incidents that are enabled or caused by human beings without malicious intent. It facilitates a qualitative assessment of these threats by analyzing the inherent qualities of actors and the work environment.

The **natural threat** component focuses on non-manmade incidents caused by biological, geological, seismic, hydrologic, or meteorological conditions or processes in the natural environment. It leverages existing measurement scales from recognized organizations (e.g., the National Oceanic and Atmospheric Administration, the Federal Emergency Management Agency, and the Centers for Disease Control) to identify and measure the severity and likelihood of natural threats to affect the critical IT Sector functions and subfunctions.

Figure 3-1: ITSRA Threat Analysis

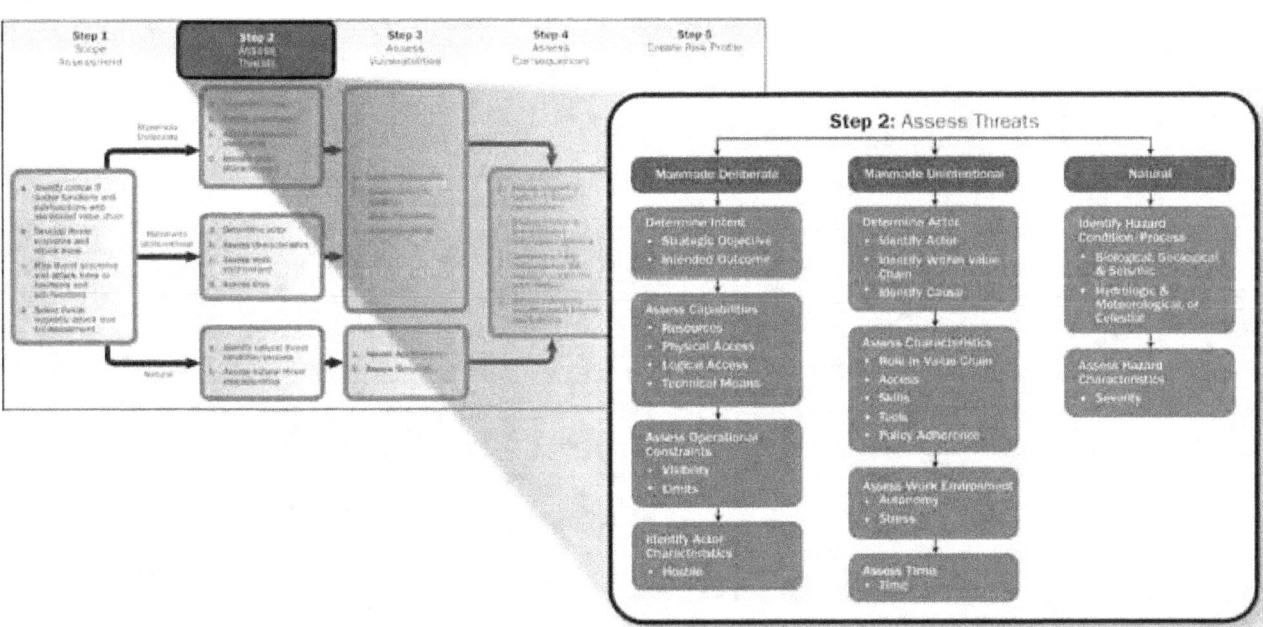

3.2.2 Assessing Vulnerabilities

The vulnerability assessment approach considers the people, process, technology, and physical vulnerabilities that, if exploited by a threat, could affect the confidentiality, integrity, or availability of critical functions. These vulnerabilities are:

- **People:** Vulnerabilities associated with critical knowledge of functions, workforce resources susceptible to intentional threats, and social aspects of infrastructure protection. This category considers factors affecting the workforce, such as human resource practices (e.g., personnel security), demographics (e.g., citizenship, qualifications), training and education (e.g., quality and quantity of institutions that teach and train the workforce), and market environments (e.g., compensation and benefits).

- **Processes:** Vulnerabilities associated with the sequence and management of operations or activities. This category includes factors such as manufacturing, logistics, and information flow (e.g., quantity and throughput of distribution channels), contingency planning and process flexibility (e.g., continuity of operations), and efficiency and effectiveness (e.g., information access globalization).

- **Technologies:** Vulnerabilities associated with integration of technologies in critical functions. This category includes factors such as reliance on hardware and software (e.g., availability and security) and system dependencies and interdependencies. When identifying vulnerabilities, the sector's approach also assesses the likelihood that the threat scenario will successfully exploit a vulnerability. To ensure a valid assessment of likelihood, the assessment considers the effectiveness of existing mitigations. This process assists the sector in determining where vulnerabilities have been addressed already and where additional mitigations may be appropriate.

- **Physical:** Vulnerabilities associated with the physical characteristics of facilities or locations. This category includes geographical location, weather, and natural vulnerabilities, such as earthquakes, floods, and other natural disaster vulnerabilities. When analyzing physical vulnerabilities, the sector's approach will assess the likelihood that a physical vulnerability could present an opportunity for people, processes, or technology to exploit a resource.

The approaches for assessing vulnerabilities of manmade deliberate and unintentional threats are similar and use four consistent criteria, as shown in figure 3-2.

Figure 3-2: ITSRA Vulnerability Analysis

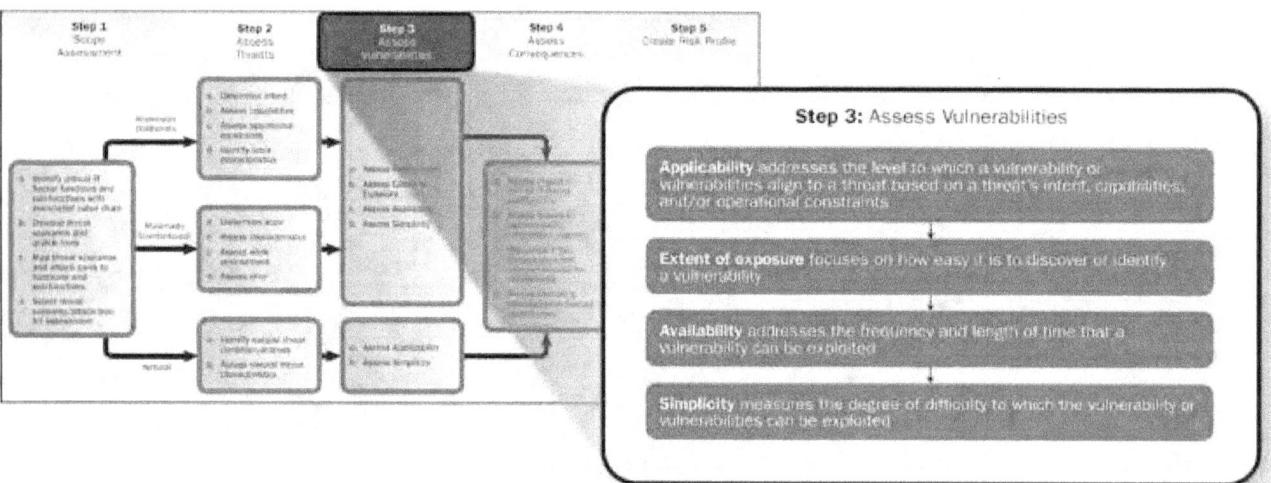

The factors associated with each threat type vary slightly because the extent of exposure and availability are not measurable factors when assessing vulnerabilities to natural threats. In addition, the vulnerability factors determine the nature of vulnerability in the infrastructure in isolation (simplicity and availability) and the relationship between the threat and the vulnerability (applicability and extent of exposure).

3.2.3 Assessing Consequences

The potential consequences to the IT Sector represent the expected range of direct and indirect impacts that could occur if a threat exploits unmitigated vulnerabilities in critical IT Sector functions. The interdependency between the physical and cyber elements of the infrastructure is of particular concern for public and private IT Sector partners. In addition, dependencies and interdependencies between and among critical IT Sector functions are evaluated and factored in future sector risk assessment efforts, as shown in figure 3-3.

Figure 3-3: ITSRA Consequence Analysis

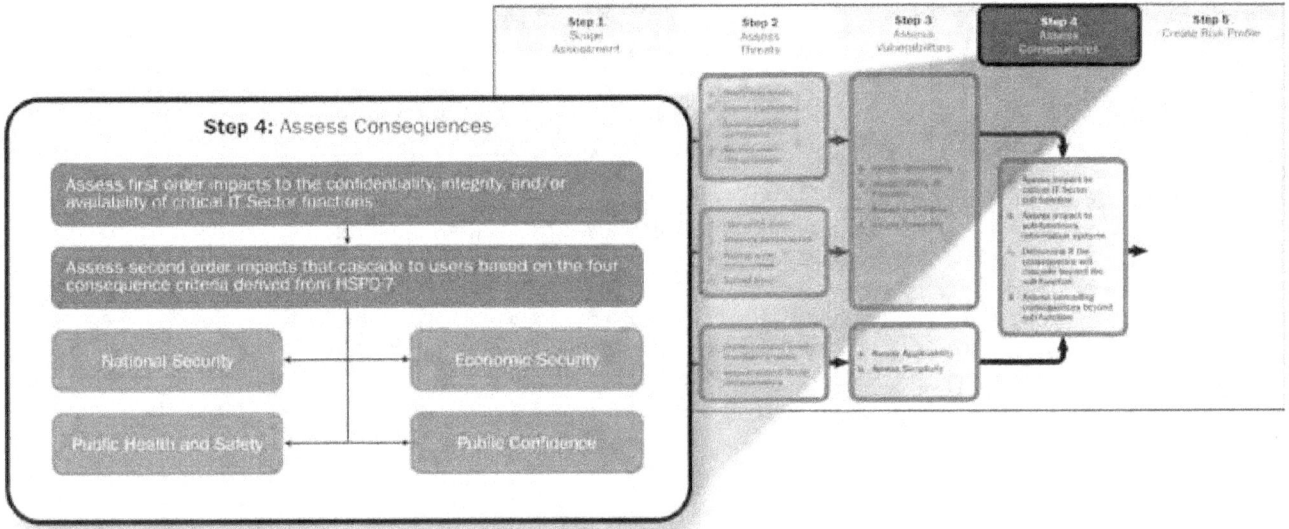

The sector's consequence framework is common to all threat types (i.e., deliberate, unintentional, and natural). Using HSPD-7 consequence categories and criteria for evaluating nationally significant events, the IT Sector's approach to consequence assessment identifies impacts on national and economic security and public health, safety, and confidence if a critical function is disrupted or degraded. The assessment considers questions such as "If this function is disrupted or degraded":

- What is the potential for loss of life, injuries, or adverse impact on public health and safety?

- How many users could be severely affected?

- What are the economic impacts, including asset replacement, business interruption, and remediation costs?

- Will Federal, State, or local governments be adversely affected? If yes, how much time might elapse before the impact is realized?

- What is the maximum amount of time that the function or process can be disrupted or degraded and still meet the minimal needed functionality in a timely manner?

- Is it possible to switch to alternate sources? If yes, how much time is required?

Private sector partners collaborated to identify the most appropriate methods for evaluating functions' consequences for their organizations and how best to share the relevant findings with the public sector partners. Similarly, public sector partners collaborated to evaluate functions' consequences from a government perspective. The results of these evaluations were combined to understand the overall impacts to the infrastructure.

3.3 IT Sector Risk Profile

Using the threat, vulnerability, and consequence frameworks in the sector's risk assessment methodology, SMEs developed a comprehensive baseline IT Sector risk profile that identified risks of concern for the sector. These risks offer the greatest confidentiality, integrity, or availability concerns to the critical functions. Table 3-1 summarizes the IT Sector's risks of concern.[9]

Table 3-1: Baseline ITSRA Risks of Concern

IT Sector Critical Function	Risks of Concern
Produce and provide IT products and services	Production or distribution of untrustworthy critical product or service through a successful manmade deliberate attack on a supply chain vulnerability.
Provide domain name resolution services	Breakdown of a single interoperable Internet through a manmade attack, and resulting failure of governance policy; large-scale manmade Denial-of-Service attack on the DNS infrastructure.
Provide Internet-based content, information, and communications services	Manmade unintentional incident caused in Internet content services results in a significant loss of e-Commerce capabilities.
Provide Internet routing, access, and connection services	Partial or complete loss of routing capabilities through a manmade deliberate attack on the Internet routing infrastructure.
Provide incident management capabilities	Impact to detection capabilities because of a lack of data availability resulting from a natural threat.

3.4 Identifying and Analyzing Interdependencies

During the baseline ITSRA, IT Sector partners also identified other infrastructure sectors on which the IT Sector relies. Sector partners identified the interdependencies among six critical IT Sector functions. As noted in the ITSRA, dependencies and interdependencies across all infrastructures should be identified and analyzed. The IT Sector is sharing its approach for dependency identification and its utility with other sectors for their own risk analysis and management efforts. In addition, broader national-level interdependency analyses are conducted by enhancing the modeling and simulation capabilities of national laboratories and government agencies.

The cross-functional analysis conducted in ITSRA provides an initial evaluation of the extent that each function depends on the other functions. As illustrated in figure 3-4, some functions were more specialized than others were, and some had broader applications to operations in cyberspace and critical infrastructures. Some functions, such as *Produce and Provide IT Products and Services*, were so broad that practically any IT Sector operation had some kind of dependency on it. Other functions, such as *Provide Incident Management Capabilities*, were so incident-specific that under normal operational conditions, no function would be dependent.

[9] Note: The baseline ITSRA did not develop risks of concern for the Identity Management function. Public and private IT Sector partners identified this as an area that requires additional study before determining the overall risk to this critical IT Sector function, and they are planning to address this concern during the next iteration of the ITSRA.

Figure 3-4: Cross-Functional Interdependencies

First Order - Exploited Function	Cross-Functional Impact						Highlighted Interdependencies
	Products & Services	Internet Routing	DNS	Identity Mgmt	Internet Content	Incident Mgmt	
Products & Services	X	High	High	High	High	High	All functions depend on **Products and Services**
Internet Routing	Medium	X	High	High	High	High	**Internet Routing** is the most basic function of the internet, thus **DNS** is highly reliant on it
DNS	Low	High	X	High	High	Medium → High	**DNS** makes **Internet Content** accessible to the average user
Identity Mgmt	Medium → High	Low	Low	X	High	Low → Medium	**Identity Management** provides security for **Internet Content**
Internet Content	Medium	Low	Low	Low	X	Medium → High	**Incident Management** relies on **Internet Content** to provide critical communication and collaboration services
Incident Mgmt	Low → High	Low → High	Low → High	Low → High	Low → High	X	All functions rely on **Incident Management** for passive and active risk mitigation

High, Medium, and Low are used to indicate the relative level of dependency across the critical IT Sector functions.

The main purpose of the interdependency analysis is to indicate the functions that were dependent on other functions, and rate whether that dependency was high, medium, or low. Recognizing the need for further analysis on dependencies and interdependencies, sector partners plan to focus subsequent risk assessment efforts on dependencies and interdependencies with other CIKR sectors and use the outcomes of the forthcoming Cyber Storm III exercise to examine cascading effects across sectors.

4. Risk Response and Management Efforts

4.1 Using the Risk Profile to Inform Mitigation Prioritization

The baseline ITSRA identified and prioritized risks of concern (see section 3.3) to the critical IT Sector functions. Using the risks identified in the ITSRA, the IT Sector will identify appropriate risk responses for these risks, and where necessary, also define and propose mitigation strategies to reduce national level risks. IT Sector partners are faced with several risk response options:

- **Risk Avoidance** involves methods to decrease the likelihood of occurrence by removing a hazard or ending a specific exposure.

- **Risk Acceptance** refers to dealing with a risk when or after it occurs. When the cost of insuring against a risk is greater over time than the potential total loss, accepting the risk is the most viable strategy.

- **Risk Mitigation** involves methods that reduce the severity of the loss or decrease the likelihood of the loss occurring.

- **Risk Transfer** can be best described as a shifting of risk from one entity to another. When a risk occurs, the losses are absorbed by another entity. Risk transfer can also refer to the spreading of losses over the entire IT Sector instead of a particular group in the IT Sector taking the entire loss.

Potential risk responses include a wide array of possible solutions and may involve assuming less likely and less consequential risks; improving physical security; establishing logical, electronic, or cyber access controls; or neutralizing threats before they can be launched against physical and cyber infrastructure assets. Identifying risk responses and prioritizing the mitigations for identified IT Sector risks helps ensure that resources are applied where they can most effectively respond to the threats, vulnerabilities, and consequences facing the critical IT Sector functions. Figure 4-1 illustrates the IT Sector's approach to risk mitigation prioritization.

The following sections describe how the process facilitates the IT Sector's risk management and prioritization activities.

Figure 4-1: IT Mitigation Prioritization Methodology

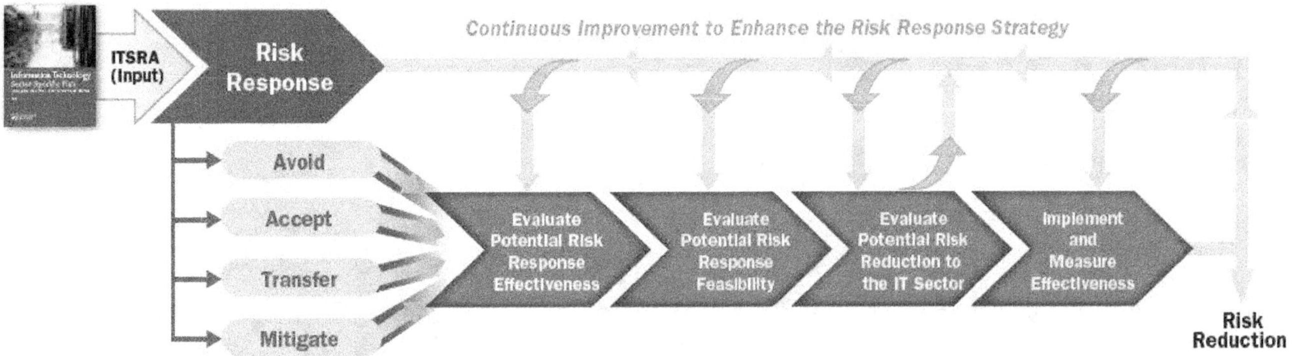

4.2 Identifying and Prioritizing Risk Responses

The objective of the sector's risk response and prioritization methodology is to achieve the greatest overall risk reduction by selecting the most effective risk response to functions that would have the greatest impact on sector capabilities. Beginning with the high-priority risks of concern, each ITSRA-identified risk is evaluated to determine the most feasible and effective management response to the respective risk. To determine the effectiveness of a potential risk response, IT Sector SMEs estimate the level to which each risk is most likely to be reduced.

The combination of the estimated effectiveness and feasibility factors for each potential risk response are evaluated to determine which risk response is most appropriate. Often, a risk response that offers the highest risk reduction may not present the most appropriate response for the IT Sector because it may not be feasible. Thus, a less effective risk response with a higher feasibility may present the best option.

This approach guides the decisionmaking process of selecting a risk response by explicitly linking each risk to a potential response, allowing sector partners to prioritize the risks identified in the ITSRA and identify the most effective methods of mitigating those risks.

After the appropriate risk response is identified for a specific risk of concern to a function, sector partners determine if implementing this response would impact (positively or negatively) the overall sector risk profile or if it impacts other critical IT Sector functions' risk profiles. If the sector partners determine that implementation of the respective risk response does not adversely affect other functions' risk profiles or that of the overall sector, then the risk response is implemented. If it is determined that a risk response would negatively impact the sector's or functions' risk profiles, then an alternative risk response approach will be identified.

After the risk response is deemed to be appropriate (i.e., effective as well as feasible) and it is not expected to adversely impact the sector- or function-level risk profiles, IT Sector partners will identify metrics to measure the overall risk reduction of a particular risk response and monitor if the response approach and strategy should be adapted.

5. Protective Programs and Resiliency Strategies

Protective programs are measures or activities that are undertaken to prepare for, prevent, protect against, respond to, and recover from incidents that have the potential to impact critical IT Sector functions. Programs are sponsored and led by public or private sector partners, or they represent a partnership between the public and private sectors.

5.1 Determining Protective Program Needs

The ITSRA illustrates the threats, vulnerabilities, and consequences facing the critical IT Sector functions. As such, ITSRA results directly inform IT Sector RMAs—namely protective programs and R&D. The goal of RMA implementation is to reduce risk to the IT Sector critical functions through protective programs and the application of the results of R&D efforts.

As referenced in section 4, sector SMEs identify risks to the critical functions against existing IT Sector protective programs to determine if:

- Existing IT Sector RMAs can adequately mitigate identified risks;
- Modifications to existing RMAs are necessary to mitigate identified risks;
- New RMAs are necessary to mitigate identified risks; or
- R&D initiatives are necessary to develop new capabilities and technologies to mitigate identified risks.

IT Sector SMEs with specific expertise on the identified risks to the critical functions evaluate specific risk mitigation requirements to develop RMA recommendations. To develop specific actions for each protective program, the IT Sector partners draw on industry and government experts associated with each protective program category. This group of SMEs is charged with the evaluation of existing protective programs. The programs are evaluated based on the effectiveness and applicability of each program relative to risk mitigation needs across the sector. If gaps arise between risk mitigation needs and existing protective programs, the IT Sector partners work to determine if the risk can be mitigated by an R&D effort, or if a new protective program is necessary to mitigate the risk.

5.2 Current IT Sector Protective Programs

As part of the NIPP risk management framework, IT Sector SMEs identified key RMAs that address the risks of concern identified in the ITSRA. Table 5-1 lists the IT Sector's key RMAs for each function and risk.

Table 5-1: Description of IT Sector RMAs[a]

		Key RMA	**Supply chain resilience and process controls** -*Existing Mitigation*
Produce and Provide IT Products and Services	**1**	**Description of Activity**	**2009 ITSRA Identified Risk:** Production or distribution of untrustworthy critical product/service through a successful manmade deliberate attack on a supply chain vulnerability *(Consequence: High; Likelihood: Low).* **Existing Mitigation Activities:** Many software and hardware manufacturers have redundancy throughout their supply chains, thereby preventing possible local and regional vulnerabilities from cascading to sector-wide events. Supply chain vulnerabilities are typically mitigated by robust and repeatable controls, as well as practices and processes that include mechanisms for updates and revisions to address the changing threat landscape. These controls, practices, and processes can be unique to the particular region in which they are performed or they can be driven by the types of operations being performed. Business continuity and contingency planning also enable producers and providers to recover or reconstitute as quickly as possible in an attack or outage. Furthermore, an adequate supply of raw materials is essential for just-in-time manufacturing of critical IT products. The sector carefully monitors the availability and quality of critical raw materials relative to demand to promote supply chain resilience.
		Key RMA	**Supply chain security and integrity** -*Existing Mitigation*
	2	**Description of Activity**	**2009 ITSRA Identified Risk:** Production or distribution of untrustworthy critical product/service through a successful manmade deliberate attack on a supply chain vulnerability *(Consequence: High; Likelihood: Low).* **Existing Mitigation Activities:** IT Sector partners employ several practices to mitigate supply chain risks including employee screening to mitigate insider threats, product development quality control processes, reviews and testing of products during the various developmental and production stages, and the use of anti-counterfeiting measures including tamper-proof labels, chips, and code. Furthermore, IT Sector partners engage with law enforcement to investigate supply chain threats, vulnerabilities, and incidents, and many partners feature Product Security Incident Response capabilities to mitigate incidents following product delivery.
Provide Domain Name Resolution Services	**3**	Key RMA	**Internet operations quality assurance and continuous monitoring** -*Existing Mitigation*
		Description of Activity	**2009 ITSRA Identified Risk:** Breakdown of a single interoperable Internet through a manmade attack, and resulting failure of governance policy *(Consequence: High; Likelihood: Medium)*; and large-scale manmade Denial-of-Service attack on the Domain Name System (DNS) infrastructure *(Consequence: High; Likelihood: Low).* **Existing Mitigation Activities:** Current mitigation strategies to prevent the breakdown of key network components in the Internet infrastructure include the continuous real-time monitoring of production equipment by network operations centers to anticipate and protect Internet infrastructure from erroneous or malicious configuration changes. Mitigations currently in place include process checks to avoid deployment of detrimental code and requiring multiple authentications for the deployment of production code.

Provide Domain Name Resolution Services (cont.)	4	**Key RMA**	Internet operations diversity and redundancy -*Existing Mitigation*
		Description of Activity	**2009 ITSRA Identified Risks:** Breakdown of a single interoperable Internet through a manmade attack, and resulting failure of governance policy *(Consequence: High; Likelihood: Medium)*; and large-scale manmade Denial-of-Service attack on the DNS infrastructure *(Consequence: High; Likelihood: Low)*.
			Existing Mitigation Activities: The DNS servers that maintain the DNS root and many of the top-level domains (TLDs) are distributed around the globe. Because DNS is a distributed system, an attack on one part of it would not necessarily paralyze the system. Furthermore, the use of Anycast, a networking and routing scheme featuring a one-to-one-to-many association between network addresses and network endpoints, mitigates the degraded performance from distributed Denial-of-Service (DDoS) attacks by facilitating availability and load balancing.
Provide Internet-based Content, Information, and Communications Services	5	**Key RMA**	Policy and access controls -*Existing Mitigation*
		Description of Activity	**2009 ITSRA Identified Risks:** Manmade unintentional incident caused in Internet content services results in a significant loss of e-Commerce capabilities *(Consequence: High; Likelihood: Negligible)*.
			Existing Mitigation Activities: The proper implementation of policy and access controls provides the most widely available mitigation for threats to the Provide Internet-based Content function. Terminating access rights immediately after an individual leaves an organization is a common mitigation currently implemented within the function. Failure to terminate access leaves the organization vulnerable to information disclosure, the introduction of malicious content, or to a brute force attack against the organization's infrastructure. The termination of access rights provides a simple and effective way to mitigate the potential vulnerabilities posed by an individual leaving an organization.
	6	**Key RMA**	Security training for users and small businesses -*Mitigation Being Enhanced*
		Description of Activity	**2009 ITSRA Identified Risks:** Manmade unintentional incident caused in Internet content services results in a significant loss of e-Commerce capabilities *(Consequence: High; Likelihood: Negligible)*.
			Risk Mitigation Activities Being Enhanced: Proper and consistent security training, both at the national and organizational level, mitigates many of the threats posed to information systems and critical infrastructure. IT Sector partners employ enterprise-level security awareness to employees to promote a security-conscious workforce. Awareness training is complemented by in house or external (e.g., SANS Institute, certification organizations) technical training to promote specific IT security skills. In addition to specific security training, several national-level cybersecurity awareness programs and organizations, such as the National Cyber Security Alliance, seek to educate and inform home users and small businesses about the importance and impact of cybersecurity.
	7	**Key RMA**	Enhance rerouting capabilities of the Communications and IT Sectors -*Potential Future Mitigation*
		Description of Activity	**2009 ITSRA Identified Risk:** Manmade unintentional incident caused in Internet content services results in a significant loss of e-Commerce capabilities *(Consequence: High; Likelihood: Negligible)*.
			Potential Future Risk Mitigation Activities: Both the IT and Communications Sectors continue to work together to provide alternative means to quickly redirect Internet traffic during an outage to ensure the constant availability of the function for all users.

		Key RMA	Enhanced routers (i.e., increased speed, reliability, and capacity of routers and router software) -*Existing Mitigation*
	8	Description of Activity	**2009 ITSRA Identified Risk:** Partial or complete loss of routing capabilities through a manmade deliberate attack on the Internet routing infrastructure *(Consequence: High; Likelihood: Low)*.
			Existing Mitigation Activities: The dramatic increase in Internet traffic has prompted router manufacturers to increase the speed, reliability, and capacity of their routers and router software, promoting increased uptime and resilience.
		Key RMA	**Ability to mitigate disruptions to Internet access** -*Mitigation Being Enhanced*
	9	Description of Activity	**2009 ITSRA Identified Risk:** Partial or complete loss of routing capabilities through a manmade deliberate attack on the Internet routing infrastructure *(Consequence: High; Likelihood: Low)*.
			Risk Mitigation Activities Being Enhanced: Organizations that are responsible for Internet routing protocols, Internet Protocol (IP) address assignment, and backbone communications engineering continue to respond to the challenges of handling the rapid increase in Internet traffic by devising standards, technologies, and techniques to make the Internet more resilient to failure. As noted in the 2009 ITSRA, the Internet Engineering Task Force (IETF) establishes standards and best practices and the American Registry for Internet Numbers (ARIN) promotes efficient assignment of IP address blocks, which reduces the size of Internet routing tables. Other operating groups are set up just for Internet Service Providers (ISPs), such as Network Service Provider Security Forum (NSP-sec) lists.
		Key RMA	**Physical security of Network Access Points (NAP) and Internet Exchange Points (IXP)** -*Mitigation Being Enhanced*
	10	Description of Activity	**2009 ITSRA Identified Risk:** Partial or complete loss of routing capabilities through a manmade deliberate attack on the Internet routing infrastructure *(Consequence: High; Likelihood: Low)*.
			Risk Mitigation Activities Being Enhanced: NAPs and IXPs continue to enhance and increase their security. The owners and operators of these facilities regularly collaborate with government to address the changing and evolving risk landscapes at each facility.
		Key RMA	**Improved routing incident response** -*Mitigation Being Enhanced*
	11	Description of Activity	**2009 ITSRA Identified Risk:** Partial or complete loss of routing capabilities through a manmade deliberate attack on the Internet routing infrastructure *(Consequence: High; Likelihood: Low)*.
			Risk Mitigation Activities Being Enhanced: Network operators and ISPs have tools, techniques, and skilled in-house security teams to monitor networks, identify incidents, and respond. Major ISPs do take precautions to prevent disruption of operations support and incident management and response. Most major providers have several backups for all of their routers, so if one router goes offline, it causes an immediate failover.

Provide Internet Routing, Access, and Connection Services

Provide Incident Management Capabilities	12	Key RMA	National-level incident response and coordination capabilities -*Existing Mitigation*
		Description of Activity	**2009 ITSRA Identified Risk:** Impact to detection capabilities due to lack of data availability resulting from a natural threat *(Consequence: High; Likelihood: Medium).*
			Existing Mitigation Activities: Entities that provide national-level incident response capabilities regularly share technical and strategic threat and vulnerability information and mitigate overall risks to existing or potential incidents. Examples of national-level incident response capabilities include the United States Computer Emergency Readiness Team (US-CERT) and the IT-ISAC, as well as working groups that address cross-sector cyber infrastructure issues, including the Cross-Sector Cyber Security Working Group and the ISAC Council. These mechanisms can also take the form of training and awareness programs to educate government and industry of likely future incidents. Furthermore, IT Sector partners are actively involved in planning for and testing national-level incident response capabilities. For example, the CyberStorm III Exercise, occurring in 2010, will test the National Cyber Incident Response Plan (NCIRP) and the National Level Exercise (NLE) 2010 will also test response and coordination. Finally, there is also a concerted effort between industry and government to integrate private sector representation through the ISACs into the National Cybersecurity and Communications Integration Center (NCCIC) which would also improve coordination during an incident.
	13	Key RMA	Distributed infrastructure and workforce -*Existing Mitigation*
		Description of Activity	**2009 ITSRA Identified Risks:** Impact to detection capabilities due to lack of data availability resulting from a natural threat *(Consequence: High; Likelihood: Medium).*
			Existing Mitigation Activities: In addition to redundant infrastructure and continuous monitoring, detection, and response capabilities, the providers' IT products and services have geographically dispersed workforces and resources.
	14	Key RMA	Information sharing enhancements creating common situational awareness -*Existing Mitigation*
		Description of Activity	**2009 ITSRA Identified Risk:** Impact to detection capabilities due to lack of data availability resulting from a natural threat *(Consequence: High; Likelihood: Medium).*
			Existing Mitigation Activities: Cyber threat and vulnerability information sharing occurs within the industry at regional, national, and international levels. Organizations such as the IT-ISAC, the Industry Consortium for the Advancement of Security on the Internet (ICASI) and the Forum of Incident Response and Security Teams (FIRST) provide forums and venues for sharing best practices, cyber intelligence, and situational awareness related information. Also, the current National Security Telecommunications Advisory Committee (NSTAC) Joint Industry Coordination Center Pilot involves information sharing between the IT, Communications, Defense Industrial Base, and Banking and Finance Sectors to improve situational awareness. In addition, ad hoc collaborative industry groups form to work common problems such as the Conficker Working Group. Furthermore, several current information-sharing programs (e.g., US-CERT) are being enhanced to better integrate the private sector into ongoing Federal cybersecurity programs.

[a] Table 5-1 lists RMAs for five of the IT Sector's six critical functions. During the ITSRA, IT Sector SMEs determined that additional analysis would be required before arriving at RMAs for Identity Management.

5.3 Creating New Protective Programs

The IT Sector RMAs listed in table 5-1 are not static; they are anticipated to change and evolve over time in concert with the sector's changing landscape. To stay abreast of current RMA needs, IT Sector partners gather the information necessary to determine whether a protective program must be created or enhanced to mitigate specific high priority risks while related R&D efforts can be identified and evaluated. Through coordination with other entities, such as the Cyber Security Information Assurance Interagency Working Group, which communicates ongoing R&D efforts related to cybersecurity sponsored by various government agencies, IT Sector partners can maintain awareness of cybersecurity R&D efforts that could impact protective program implementation and decisionmaking in the IT Sector.

IT Sector working groups promote regular interactions between public and private sector entities in the IT Sector. By regularly convening to share key RMA information, industry partners collaborate with the government to limit duplicative efforts and share protective program workloads. This effort ensures that a line of communication remains open between the government and private sector to coordinate an organized response to cybersecurity threats that affect the sector as a whole.

5.4 Monitoring Program Implementation and Effectiveness

After a new or existing protective program is identified, IT Sector SMEs evaluate its potential effectiveness and feasibility (see section 4.3). Following implementation, IT Sector SMEs then evaluate its actual effectiveness. IT Sector partners develop outcome-based metrics for each IT Sector function to determine the effectiveness of the RMAs (see chapter 6). Using an outcome-based approach enables IT Sector partners to monitor threats to each function over time and make risk-based protective program implementation and modification decisions. This cyclical approach helps ensure that the RMAs continue to evolve and change over time in support of new risks identified in subsequent ITSRAs. IT Sector partners also make recommendations about changes to protective programs through the annual IT Sector Annual Report (SAR).

6. Measure Effectiveness

As noted in chapter 1, the IT Sector is composed of virtual and distributed functions necessary to provide IT products and services. These critical IT Sector functions are provided by a combination of entities that provide hardware, software, IT systems, and services. Rather than focus on individual assets, the IT Sector's risk assessment methodology focuses on assessing national-level risks to the critical functions. Results from the ITSRA inform protective program and R&D priorities to mitigate risks to the sector's critical functions. With critical functions serving as the foundation of the IT Sector's risk management approach, the sector's measurement methodology relies on a functions-based approach to analyze the effectiveness of its efforts to mitigate CIKR risks, plus promote protection and resilience.

6.1 Risk Mitigation Activities

As referenced in chapter 5, IT Sector partners rely on several key RMAs to mitigate risk and promote protection and resilience efforts. Most of the sector's RMAs focus on maintaining and enhancing an effective public-private partnership to:

- Share cybersecurity and IT Sector CIKR protection information; and,

- Promote recovery and reconstitution of critical IT Sector services and functions.

The IT Sector's key RMAs are presented in table 5-1.

6.2 Process for Measuring Progress and Effectiveness

IT Sector SMEs conduct efforts to identify and implement outcome-based metrics to determine if the IT Sector's RMAs are adequately mitigating risks facing the critical functions as intended. For new RMA recommendations, IT Sector partners establish metrics that can be used to evaluate the implementation progress and post-implementation effectiveness of each newly proposed RMA over time. This combination of implementation-level working group analysis and outcome-based measurement is used to determine risk mitigation efficacy. IT Sector partner oversight and aggregation across the sector help ensure that the RMAs accurately reflect needed capabilities to promote sector security and resilience.

Metrics enable partners to monitor the status of risk mitigation activities and facilitate improvement in the security and resilience of IT CIKR by applying corrective actions based on observed measurements. Metrics assist IT Sector partners in answering fundamental questions (see table 6-1) that help guide risk management activities. To answer these questions, sector partners work to identify status and outcome metrics to describe the progress in analyzing risk reduction activities and the resulting effectiveness of the IT Sector RMAs and security initiatives.

Table 6-1: IT Sector Metrics

	Metric Type	Question	Metric Purpose
Easier to answer	Risk Response Activity (RRA) Status	Is the IT Sector analyzing potential responses to the risks identified in the ITSRA and making informed risk response decisions?	**RRA Metrics:** these metrics report the administrative progress of ITSRA risk response analysis and decisions. **Example Status Metric:** % of ITSRA risks for which risk response has been identified
	RMA Status/ Progress	Is the IT Sector effectively developing and implementing RMAs to reduce risks to the sector's critical functions?	**RMA Status Metrics:** these metrics report the administrative status of RMA development activities, implementation decisions, and implementation progress. **Example Status Metric:** % of RMA implementations completed
Harder to answer	RMA Security Outcome	What is the measurable impact of implemented RMAs on the security, assurance, and resilience of the IT Sector's critical functions?	**RMA Outcome Metrics:** Where possible, outcome data evaluates the *actual security impact/outcome* of an RMA implementation. In cases where the RMA has not reached a maturity level where it is producing measurable outcomes, the IT Sector will identify an outcome metric and plan to collect data for the metric after the RMA reaches a mature state. **Example Outcome Metric:** Annual % increase/decrease in security incidents causing > $1M loss

While status and progress metrics provide useful indicators for process implementation and efficiency, outcome measures are the preferred means to determine risk mitigation effectiveness across the IT Sector. These metrics provide evidence of risk mitigation impact; however, while outcome measures enable the IT Sector to demonstrate the impact of its RMAs, they are not possible in all situations and are often more difficult to identify and quantify. Consequently, sector partners identify status and outcome metrics to describe the progress of analyzing IT Sector risks, developing RMAs to mitigate risks, and the resulting effectiveness of the IT Sector RMAs.

6.2.1 Process for Measuring Sector Progress

Outcome metrics provide the primary method of measuring the effectiveness of existing and future strategies designed to mitigate the risks identified in the current and future versions of the ITSRA. IT Sector partners are working together to prioritize risk mitigation strategies based on the outcomes of the ITSRA. This process includes a review of existing R&D and protective program initiatives, including components of the U.S. Government's cyber RMAs.

To measure progress against the baseline ITSRA, IT Sector partners:

• Evaluate the ITSRA-identified risks, beginning with high-consequence, high-likelihood risks, across the six critical functions and the potential mitigation strategies associated with each specific risk; and

• Conduct a risk reduction activity analysis to determine if the risk should be mitigated, avoided, accepted, or transferred.

RRA status metrics enable sector partners to track progress on addressing the risks identified in the ITSRA. If sector partners determine to mitigate the risk, they will evaluate the estimated effect of each potential mitigation strategy to determine which strategies will result in the greatest net impact to risk reduction. As referenced in chapter 4, IT Sector SMEs will combine each mitigation activity's relative effectiveness and feasibility rankings to arrive at an overall ranking for each potential risk mitigation activity. Armed with this prioritized information, IT Sector SMEs can focus on those RMAs that, through implementation of the related mitigation, provide a measurable reduction in the associated risk's likelihood, vulnerability, and consequence factors.

IT Sector SMEs can then develop implementation plans for each RMA and sector partners can develop progress and outcome-based metrics to monitor the RMA's status and effectiveness through completion. These measures will be validated by subsequent assessments to determine if the RMA is, indeed, resulting in the forecast risk reduction across the sector. This outcome-driven, integrated measurement approach enables the IT Sector to continuously monitor its risk posture relative to its national-level critical functions. The collaboration between IT Sector partners also promotes an agile, measurement-driven approach to risk-based decisionmaking across the IT Sector.

6.2.2 Information Collection and Verification

The RMAs form the basis of IT Sector measurement. During the metrics development process for each RMA, members of IT Sector working groups, owners, operators, and responsible parties associated with each RMA identify points of contact to determine:

- Metrics to produce meaningful approximations of risk reduction progress;
- Data needed to compute each metric;
- Data availability;
- Data validity; and
- Appropriate periodicity for data collection to yield meaningful results.

Sector partners work with the identified points of contact to collect and report metrics data based on the periodicity prescribed with each metric.

6.2.3 Reporting

The IT Sector relies on the NIPP SAR process to report and share relevant metrics data for IT Sector RMAs. Before the IT SAR is finalized, all IT SCC and IT GCC members have an opportunity to review the report to evaluate the accuracy and relevance of the data and offer concurrence.

In addition to the formal SAR process, IT Sector working groups meet regularly to review RMA needs and progress based on the sector's measurement approach, described in section 6.2.1. These meetings promote information sharing and performance monitoring among all partners across the sector.

6.3 Using Metrics for Continuous Improvement

The IT Sector's measurement approach promotes continuous improvement by using the data garnered from measurement efforts to inform risk-reducing protective program implementations and R&D investments. Furthermore, because the IT Sector's metrics approach is informed by the ITSRA, and subsequent assessments will be used to evaluate the sector's risk reduction and resilience progress, the sector's measurement approach uses past results to inform future planning and directly supports the NIPP risk management framework.

7. CIKR Protection R&D

7.1 Overview of Sector R&D

The IT Sector operates by a slightly different paradigm than the other CIKR sectors. While the government invests a substantial amount of resources in cybersecurity CIKR R&D, the private sector also makes significant contributions. The continuous process of innovation in the private sector fuels new products and capabilities that establish competitive differentiation among the private sector entities. While the private sector entities are willing to support the collaborative nature of such efforts, it is important that such collaboration not compromise the competitive positions of the participants. Consequently, R&D collaboration efforts should ensure:

- The public sector benefits by prioritizing limited government R&D funds toward initiatives that are not significantly prioritized by the private sector; and,

- The private sector benefits by participation in the end-to-end risk management process through visibility into the national cyber CIKR needs, helping to prioritize private sector investments.

As the IT Sector advances its R&D agenda, it will be important for the public and private sectors to work collaboratively and share R&D information in pursuit of sector goals and objectives. Leveraging private sector R&D investment while respecting the proprietary nature of some of those efforts and sharing information on government R&D initiatives and priorities are critical to the IT Sector's overall R&D strategy.

The key to understanding the private sector role in such collaboration is to understand the two types of private sector entities that participate in cyber CIKR R&D. These are:

- **Direct R&D Beneficiaries:** Those private sector entities that derive direct financial benefit from performing R&D on behalf of public sector requirements. In other words, those entities that pursue R&D to bring new cybersecurity technology and products to market.

Figure 7-1: IT Sector R&D Process

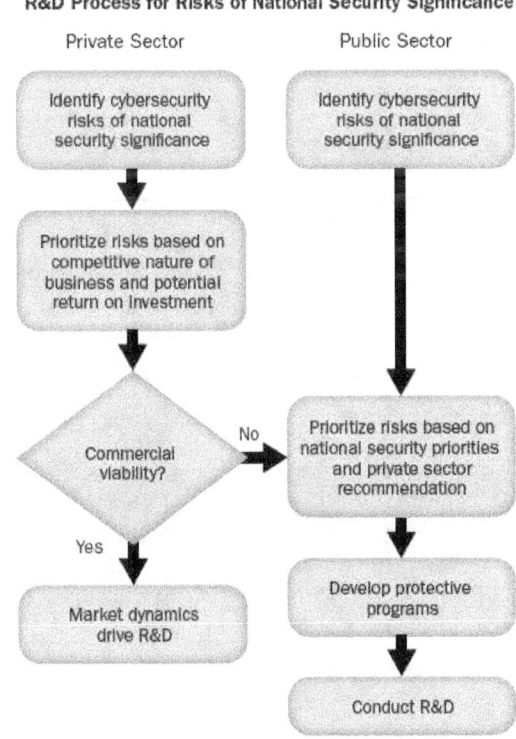

- **Indirect R&D Beneficiaries:** Those private sector entities that do not derive direct financial benefit from performing R&D speculate to develop new products for the marketplace. In other words, those entities that sell IT sector products and conduct R&D using internal funds to enhance those products.

To understand the challenge of collaboration better in this environment, the IT Sector partners visualize the role of public and private sector R&D as an ecosystem where the private sector focuses on certain portions of R&D that are commercially viable from a return-on-investment perspective. At the same time, the private sector naturally deprioritizes investments in R&D that have limited commercial viability, and these areas, if identified as high risk, should alternatively receive more attention from the Federal Government.

With competitive pressure, the private sector is less interested in openly sharing all of the areas that they are prioritizing, and even less likely, the specific work being done in each of these areas. This fact led the IT Sector partners to propose an alternate mechanism of collaboration. Private sector entities could share in areas where they are not making investment, rather than where they are making an investment, so public sector participants can still receive the benefit of collaboration without the need for private sector entities to divulge sensitive competitive information in the collaborative environment.

To continue the progress achieved since the completion of the 2007 IT SSP, the IT Sector partners continue to coordinate with government agencies involved with IT R&D. The IT Sector has developed relationships with the Office of Science and Technology Policy, DHS/IP and S&T, and the Cyber Security Information Assurance Interagency Working Group in the NITRD Program in anticipation of future collaboration on informing government R&D priorities. This expansion of coordination and collaboration is a vital step in recognizing the broad influence, investment, and need to coordinate with a broad constituent base to promote cyber CIKR R&D.

Moving forward, the IT Sector will need to continue coordination with the Communications Sector on R&D CIKR protection priorities that overlap or have inherent synergies; share results from the collaborative framework with R&D public and private sector partners; and develop a roadmap for IT Sector R&D priorities and resource needs.

The plan for completing these actions and additional activities geared toward managing risk are discussed further in subsequent sections.

7.2 Sector R&D Requirements

Currently, the IT Sector provides R&D recommendations and requirements to the Federal Government through the SAR. These recommendations are based on the previously identified priority areas. These recommendations provide the government the opportunity to focus R&D investments on critical areas that require a high level of government oversight or where viability in the commercial marketplace is limited or nonexistent. In addition, continued dialog among public and private sector partners can raise awareness of areas where the private sector has invested significant R&D resources to meet CIKR protection and cyber-security needs.

To foster improved coordination, the IT Sector partners began a review of the IT Sector's current R&D priorities in an effort to more closely align R&D priority areas with existing initiatives in the government. The CSIA IWG has adopted a set of 43 priority areas. These areas are used by all 13 Federal agencies that participate in the CSIA IWG. IT Sector partners are aligning the nine IT Sector R&D priority areas established in the 2007 IT SSP with the CSIA IWG priority areas. The adoption of the CSIA IWG priority areas as a common lexicon in the IT Sector will allow an easier transition of recommendations to the Federal Government. Table 7-1 shows the alignment of current IT Sector R&D priorities with the CSIA IWG priority areas.

Table 7-1: Alignment of IT Sector R&D Priorities

CSIA R&D Priorities	IT Sector R&D Priorities
Functional Cybersecurity and Information Assurance • Authentications, authorization, and trust management • Access control and privilege management • Attack protection, prevention, and preemption • Large-scale cyber situational awareness • Automated attack detection, warning, and response • Insider threat detection and mitigation • Detection of hidden information and covert information flows • Recovery and reconstitution • Forensics, traceback, and attribution	**Cyber Situational Awareness and Response** • Large-scale cyber situational awareness • Automated attack detection, warning, and response • Insider threat detection and mitigation • Detection of hidden information and covert information flows • Recovery and reconstitution **Forensics, Traceback, and Attribution** • Ability to track individuals and computers • Remote access to target computers • Network forensics • Evidence sampling • Prediction of error rates in analyses **Identity Management: Authentication, Authorization, and Accounting** • Device authentication • Scalable authentication
Securing the Infrastructure • Secure DNS • Secure routing protocols • IPv6, IPsec, and other Internet protocols • Secure process control systems	**Intrinsic Infrastructure Protocols Security** • Secure DNS • Secure routing protocols • IPv6, IPsec, and other Internet protocols • Secure process control systems • Domain-specific security **Control Systems Security** • Novel security properties • Security metrics • Testing and assurance • National testbed and testing program
Domain-Specific Security • Wireless security • Secure radio frequency identification • Security of converged networks and heterogeneous environments • Next-generation priority services	**Cyber Situational Awareness and Response** • Large-scale cyber situational awareness • Automated attack detection, warning, and response • Insider threat detection and mitigation • Detection of hidden information and covert information flows • Recovery and reconstitution
Cybersecurity and Information Assurance Characterization and Assessment • Software quality assessment and fault characterization • Detection of vulnerabilities and malicious code • Standards • Metrics • Software testing and assessment tools • Risk-based decisionmaking • Critical infrastructure dependencies and interdependencies	

CSIA R&D Priorities	IT Sector R&D Priorities
Foundations for Cybersecurity and Information Assurance · Hardware and firmware security · Secure operating systems · Security-centric programming languages · Security technology and policy management methods and policy specification languages · Information provenance · Information integrity · Cryptography · Multilevel security · Secure software engineering · Fault-tolerant and resilient systems · Integrated, enterprise-wide security monitoring and management · Analytical techniques for security across the IT systems engineering life cycle	**Secure Coding, Software Engineering, and Hardware Design Improvement** · Hardware and firmware security · Secure operating systems · Security-centric programming languages · Security technology and policy management · Information provenance · Information integrity · Cryptography · Multilevel security · Secure software engineering · Fault-tolerant and resilient systems · Integrated, enterprise-wide security monitoring and management · Analytical techniques
Enabling Technologies for Cybersecurity and Information Assurance R&D · Cybersecurity and information assurance R&D testbeds · IT system modeling, simulation, and visualization · Internet modeling, simulation, and visualization · Network mapping · Red teaming	**Modeling and Testing** · Cybersecurity and information assurance R&D testbeds · IT system modeling, simulation, and visualization · Internet modeling, simulation, and visualization · Network mapping · Red teaming
Advanced and Next-Generation Systems and Architectures · Trusted computing base architectures · Inherently secure, high assurance, and provably secure systems and architectures · Composable and scalable secure systems · Autonomic systems · Architectures for next-generation Internet infrastructure · Quantum cryptography	**Scalable and Composable Secure Systems** · New frameworks and architectures · Secure, composable, and scalable IT system technologies and development methodologies · Composable and scalable cybersecurity technologies
Social Dimensions of Cybersecurity and Information Assurance · Trust in the Internet · Privacy	**Trust and Privacy** · Trust in the Internet · Privacy

The IT Sector is also analyzing the risks of concern identified in the baseline ITSRA and aligning them to the 43 priority areas so that sector partners may better communicate recommendations for R&D funding. The R&D recommendations will be informed and updated by the ITSRA and provided to DHS/IP, S&T, and the broader public sector cyber CIKR R&D community through the SAR process.

7.3 Sector R&D Plan

The sector is integrating the results of the ITSRA into the IT Sector working groups for action. For the public and private sectors to successfully identify and prioritize cybersecurity R&D needs, full participation is required by both public and private sector R&D SMEs. The following activities are planned to facilitate the mitigation of risk:

- Align the risks of concern to protective program categories and R&D priority areas;

- Ensure participation of both public and private sector SMEs; and

- Provide recommendations.

7.3.1 Align ITRSA Risks of Concern to Protective Program Categories and R&D Priority Areas

The public and private sectors have similar R&D processes that can be coordinated to avoid unnecessary duplication and enable direct funding in areas of higher need. Public and private sector partners agree that a process is needed to communicate and coordinate R&D priorities. To ensure that limited resources are allocated efficiently against areas of greatest need, the following steps will inform the identification and prioritization of R&D needs:

- Leverage sector risk assessment results to further identify R&D needs;

- Evaluate known R&D initiatives and projects to determine if they meet R&D needs identified in the ITSRA; and,

- Develop a list of (1) current R&D efforts that meet the risks identified by the ITSRA and (2) needs that should be addressed by future R&D projects and initiatives.

Under the NIPP risk management framework, CIKR sectors are assessing risk to critical assets, systems, networks, and functions by considering vulnerabilities, threats, and consequences. Sectors can establish priorities based on the results of sector risk assessments and determine and implement protective programs and resiliency strategies, including R&D needs related to cybersecurity.

Using the baseline ITSRA, sector partners are currently identifying gaps and requirements for IT Sector protective programs and R&D initiatives to promote resilience and enhanced security across the sector. Specifically, members of the IT Sector will identify and make recommendations on (1) new R&D priority areas and (2) R&D needs to mitigate risk to IT Sector critical functions. Activities in support of this goal include:

- Briefing IT Sector representatives on results of the ITSRA, focusing on gaps that need to be filled to mitigate risk to the IT Sector critical functions; and,

- Facilitating discussions with IT Sector representatives and other SMEs, as appropriate, to identify new or modify existing R&D priority areas. The following questions form the foundation for a common taxonomy:

  - *How many projects are underway in pursuit of that priority?* Although quantity is not a comprehensive measure of success, it is important to track the various efforts focused on a given objective.

  - *What is the relevance of each project to the goal of the area, and to what extent does each project contribute to the solution of the problem the area identifies?* It is conceivable that some projects would be more relevant than others would. It is important to track the relevance of the projects to measure how they affect the desired outcome.

  - *Will the projects partially or completely mitigate a capability gap identified by another NIPP CIKR sector?*

  - *What is the potential for each project to result in products that can be transitioned to the field?* This is a test of the project's ability to provide practical solutions.

  - *At what technology readiness level will a project be considered complete enough to be released to the sector?* This is a measure of the current progress toward achieving the goals of the research area.

In each priority area, existing R&D initiatives and projects (both public and private sector) will be evaluated against several criteria, such as urgency, existing funding, and maturity of the effort to determine if sector needs are being met. The first step toward a clear set of recommendations will be through facilitated discussions, where public and private sector partners will provide input to inform a gap analysis of cybersecurity needs and requirements and current R&D initiatives. Information shared during these discussions will focus on highlighting activities across the IT Sector so that partners have insight rather than specifically identifying individual private sector efforts by company. If needs are not being met by existing public or private sector R&D efforts, the private sector may decide to pursue R&D in those areas or recommend to the Federal Government that attention and funding be focused on those gaps. These discussions will result in new sector capability gaps being submitted through the SAR process.

7.3.2 Ensure Participation of Both Public and Private Sector SMEs

OSTP collects a large amount of data on Federal Government R&D initiatives; however, this aggregated information is not widely available to private sector partners nor is it easily distilled into a user-friendly format. The IT Sector is researching ongoing government R&D programs to present available data on current Federal cybersecurity R&D efforts to the private sector. The presentation of current government cybersecurity R&D efforts will set the stage for an integrated review of this information. The creation of a formal forum to present current government cybersecurity R&D efforts would set the stage for an integrated review of this information.

The relationships developed between the IT Sector partners and components of DHS, such as IP, S&T, and working groups like the CSIA IWG provide support from the public sector. The IT SCC maintains a membership of knowledgeable SMEs who are committed to the mitigation of risks to CIKR. This public-private partnership will provide the participation necessary to reach this goal.

7.3.3 Provide Recommendations

In DHS, IP leads the coordinated national effort to reduce risk to CIKR sectors by increasing the Nation's level of preparedness and its ability to respond and quickly recover in an attack, natural disaster, or other emergency. IP's vision is for a transparent and repeatable R&D requirements program to mitigate long-term risks to homeland security. CIKR sector R&D requirements can be informed by an understanding of the dependency CIKR sectors have on the IT Sector and the risk of that dependency on sector operations. Where IT Sector mitigations do not exist to address risk, protective programs, R&D projects, or initiatives identified as other mission needs (OMN) may be required. Steps needed to identify these dependencies are as follows:

- Identify and prioritize cybersecurity-related R&D requirements necessary to fill gaps.

- Report identified cybersecurity-related R&D needs through the SAR process in coordination with IP and S&T.

- DHS/IP, in coordination with S&T, will track IT Sector R&D initiatives identified through the NIPP R&D process on behalf of the sector.

As part of the NIPP requirements, IP and S&T will assist SSAs and CIKR sectors with identifying and articulating R&D requirements and OMNs. CIKR sector R&D efforts and priorities are captured in SARs and incorporated into S&T R&D initiatives and projects. Sector cybersecurity R&D requirements should be identified in SARs and fed into S&T processes for identifying and addressing R&D needs. Through the CSCSWG, cross-sector cybersecurity R&D needs and requirements should be identified and recommendations made where government should make targeted investments. To reach this goal, the IT Sector needs to:

- Share recommendations on IT Sector R&D needs that the Federal Government should address with NITRD through the CSIA IWG.

- Facilitate discussions with CSCSWG members to identify cybersecurity-related R&D requirements that should be addressed by the Federal Government and share recommendations with NITRD through the CSIA IWG.

- Use IP to track capability gaps and OMNs on behalf of the IT Sector.

7.4 R&D Management Process

The Joint IT Sector Risk Management work group's activities will provide the structure and guidance to continue the risk management process. Through continued involvement with the CSIA IWG and regular R&D meetings involving DHS S&T and IP, the sector partners will strive to ensure that the sector's activities complement ongoing Federal R&D activities.

8. Managing and Coordinating SSA Responsibilities

8.1 Program Management Approach

HSPD-7 designated DHS with responsibility for managing and coordinating IT Sector CIKR protection activities, including leading the development, implementation, and maintenance of the SSP in coordination with the IT SCC and GCC. DHS delegated this responsibility to NCSD, part of DHS/CS&C.

NCSD is the Federal Government's focal point for cybersecurity coordination and preparedness. As the SSA for the IT Sector, NCSD leverages resources across all of its branches and programs to support IT Sector CIKR protection activities. NCSD's Critical Infrastructure Protection Cyber Security (CIP CS) program plays a critical role in carrying out NCSD's responsibility as the SSA for the IT Sector. In partnership with public and private sector partners, CIP CS facilitates IT Sector risk reduction through infrastructure identification, vulnerability assessment, and protective measures initiatives. The program coordinates risk management activities across the sector through participation in joint IT Sector working groups that oversee, carry out, and measure the development and implementation of the SSP. In this way, CIP CS is the primary day-to-day resource for the sector in the NIPP process.

CIP CS draws on its relationship with other NCSD programs that provide valuable information and tools to support SSP implementation. These include US-CERT, CSSP, O&A, the Cyber Exercise Program (CEP), and the Software Assurance (SwA) Program. In addition to these NCSD programs, the CIP CS Program, DHS/IP, and the Office of Intelligence and Analysis (I&A) promote shared CIKR situational awareness and protection strategies. Each of these programs has a unique mission that enhances IT Sector resilience. CIP CS regularly coordinates with these organizations to ensure the sector has adequate resources to carry out the imperatives in the SSP.

8.2 Processes and Responsibilities

8.2.1 SSP Maintenance and Updates

The IT SSP is a living document; consequently, NCSD and the IT SCC and GCC representatives will review and update it to reflect changes in the sector's security posture and programs. These updates will leverage the partnership between the IT SCC and GCC and build on the processes used to develop this plan. For example, the IT Sector Plans and Reports Working Group will continue to facilitate discussions and dialog on the IT SSP.

In addition to SSP updates, DHS triennially reviews and updates the NIPP. NCSD works closely with the IT SCC, IT GCC, and other partners to coordinate their participation in the triennial review.

HSPD-7 mandates that each sector will produce SARs to identify, prioritize, and coordinate CIKR protection in its sector. The NIPP provides additional details about these reports. The SARs describe the sector's CIKR protection goals, priorities, programs, and related funding, as well as report on CIKR protection progress. NCSD develops the IT SAR with input from the IT SCC and IT GCC to ensure that it accurately reflects the range of sector activities.

8.2.2 SSP Implementation Milestones

Table 8-1 relates significant accomplishments and planned activities for each chevron of the NIPP risk management framework.

Table 8-1: Significant Accomplishments and Planned Activities under the NIPP Framework

Chevron	Significant Accomplishments and Planned Activities
Set goals and objectives	• IT Sector partners review the sector's goals as part of annual IT SSP review process and actively track sector-wide progress against them. • The IT Sector's goals and objectives guided the development of the IT Sector risk assessment methodology and the sector's R&D collaboration framework. • The IT Sector will use its goals and objectives to guide its risk mitigation and measurement activities.
Identify assets, systems, and networks	• The IT SCC and GCC used a consensus-based approach to identify six critical functions and supporting subfunctions that are required to maintain or reconstitute networks (e.g., the Internet, local networks, and wide area networks) and are vital to national and economic security and public health, safety, and confidence. • The IT Sector screened its critical functions based on HSPD-7 consequence categories and criteria for evaluating nationally significant events.

Assess risks	• The IT Sector conducted the first-ever ITSRA in 2008 and 2009.
	• The risk assessment resulted in the identification of six risks that represent high confidentiality, integrity, or availability impacts of the critical functions:
	  – Supply chain vulnerability: Production or distribution of an untrustworthy critical product or service (Manmade Deliberate);
	  – Policy failure: Breakdown of a single, interoperable, global Internet (Manmade Deliberate);
	  – Large-scale attack on infrastructure: Denial-of-Service (Manmade Deliberate);
	  – Loss of e-Commerce (Manmade Unintentional);
	  – Partial or complete loss of routing capabilities (Manmade Deliberate); and
	  – Lack of data (Incident Management): Impact to detection (Natural).
	• Sector partners are currently using results of the baseline ITSRA to develop risk assessment methodologies to examine sector dependencies for analysis.

Prioritize	• The ITSRA resulted in a risk profile that prioritized risks to the IT Sector.
	• Sector partners are currently developing a methodology to prioritize RMAs in response to the risks identified in the ITSRA by:
	  – Evaluating the feasibility and effectiveness of proposed RMAs; and
	  – Prioritizing RMAs based on feasibility and effectiveness criteria.

Implement programs (and resilience strategies)	• Based on the results of prioritization activities, the IT Sector, in collaboration with DHS IP and S&T, works to leverage existing protective programs to mitigate applicable capability gaps and to develop new protective programs to mitigate capability gaps where R&D is either not underway or beneficial.
Measure effectiveness	• IT Sector partners track progress in implementing IT SSP action items to ensure that the sector maintains momentum on key objectives. • Sector partners are in the process of identifying sector-specific RRA and RMA status and outcome measures to evaluate progress.

8.2.3 Resources and Budgets

The ability to pursue CIKR protection activities depends on the availability and allocation of resources. Public and private IT Sector partners make investments and contribute resources (e.g., people, time, and money) to operate critical IT Sector functions and promote the resilience and security of those functions. Because of the sector's diversity and the number of partners providing resources to secure the sector, neither NCSD nor any other entity has authority over resources and budgets for the entire sector. The NIPP process is designed to prioritize programs and R&D efforts to ensure funding flows to the most critical areas of the IT Sector. The IT GCC and SCC will work together to ensure that public and private sector spending reflects the best allocation of available resources.

8.2.3.1 Managing Sector Resources

IT infrastructure owners and operators ultimately manage their own resources to secure their respective portions of the IT Sector's infrastructure. Federal, State, and local governments also manage resources to ensure the availability and resilience of government services. NCSD is responsible for managing some of the Federal Government's resources that support the CIKR protection of the sector. NCSD will work with other Federal departments and agencies, through the IT GCC, to coordinate priorities for non-SSA funding and resources that support the sector. The private sector can aid in resource allocation decisions by helping the government better understand the resource impact of CIKR protection and security demands made on the sector and the trickle-down effect on citizens and consumers. Understanding that the required levels of security investment exceed enterprise capability can help NCSD justify the allocation of resources for national-level capabilities and programs that contribute to the resilience of critical IT Sector functions.

8.2.3.2 Investment Priorities

Through the IT Sector SAR, NCSD will identify investment priorities based on risk management priorities, lessons learned, the success of protective programs, and identified needs. NCSD will compile this report in coordination with public and private sector partners. The report will include priorities and program funding for the current year and projected funding for the following year.

8.2.4 Training and Education

In addition to company and technology-specific training and education offerings from IT Sector partners, several NCSD programs fulfill NIPP risk analysis, protective measures, and partnership education, training, and outreach functions. The NCSD O&A Program promotes cybersecurity awareness among and within the general public and key communities, maintains relationships with governmental cybersecurity professionals to share information about cybersecurity initiatives, and develops partnerships to promote collaboration on cybersecurity issues. The NCSD O&A Program conducts significant cybersecurity awareness to the public during October, which is National Cybersecurity Awareness Month.

In addition, the NCSD Cyber Education and Workforce Development Program (CEWD) plays a key role in developing and improving the Nation's cybersecurity workforce by developing and integrating Federal Government and industry initiatives to promote and facilitate the availability of adequately trained cybersecurity professionals to support the Nation's cybersecurity needs through workforce development programs. CEWD's efforts help strengthen the skills of the national IT security workforce and ensure a strong and dependable pipeline of future cybersecurity professionals. Among other accomplishments, CEWD recently developed the IT Security Essential Body of Knowledge (EBK): A Competency and Functional Framework for IT Security Workforce Development. EBK is an umbrella framework that links competencies and functional perspectives to IT security roles fulfilled by personnel in the public and private sectors. Benefits of the IT Security EBK for professional development and workforce management initiatives include:

- Articulating the functions that professionals in the IT security workforce perform, in a context-neutral format and language;

- Promoting uniform competency guidelines to increase the overall efficiency of IT security training and education; and

- Providing a content guideline that can be leveraged to facilitate cost-effective professional development of the IT workforce, including future skills training and certifications, academic curricula, or other affiliated human resource activities, such as recruiting and career path planning.

CEWD cosponsors the National Centers of Academic Excellence in Information Assurance Education (CAEIAE) and CAE-Research (CAE-R) Programs with the National Security Agency (NSA). Four-year colleges and graduate-level universities adopting the Center of Academic Excellence (CAE) model curriculum and standards are eligible to apply for the CAE designation. Across the country, nearly 100 institutions are recognized as CAEs for their collective role in strengthening the current and future supply of cyber-savvy individuals in our Nation's workforce. In addition, CEWD co-sponsors the Federal Cyber Service: Scholarship for Service (SFS) Program with the National Science Foundation (NSF). The SFS program offers scholarships to outstanding undergraduate, graduate, and doctoral students in exchange for service at a Federal agency as an information assurance professional. This mutually beneficial exchange fills a critical need in our Nation's workforce.

The NCSD CEP improves the Nation's cybersecurity readiness, protection, and incident response capabilities by developing, designing, and conducting cyber exercises and workshops at the Federal, State, regional, and international level. The NCSD CEP uses scenario-based exercises that focus on risks to the cyber and IT infrastructure. Through exercises, participants can validate policies, plans, procedures, processes, and capabilities that enable preparation, prevention, response, recovery, and continuity of operations (COOP). The vast amount of public and private sector participation in the planning and execution of cyber exercises promotes partnership building by all participants and effective information sharing between the private sector and Government, consistent with NIPP CIKR competency areas.

In addition to formal DHS/NCSD programs to promote outreach, education, and awareness, the IT Sector effectively coordinates specific outreach activities through its effective public-private partnership model. For example, through coordinated outreach, the IT Sector brought together more than 50 SMEs from across government and the private sector to participate in the ITSRA. The IT Sector also developed and implemented an outreach strategy to brief all IT Sector members and IT CIKR stakeholders and partners on the results and impacts of the ITSRA.

Finally, the IT Sector features a formal meeting schedule that promotes awareness across all concerned constituencies. The IT SCC Executive Council meets biweekly to share information and drive CIKR protection activities. All public-private IT Sector implementation groups meet at least monthly. Furthermore, the IT SCC and GCC meet twice a year, the IT SCC plenary meets quarterly, and the IT Sector and Communications Sector SCCs and GCCs meet annually at the Quad meeting.[10] This aggressive meeting schedule helps ensure pertinent CIKR information is passed to all affected entities.

8.3 Implementing the Partnership Model

8.3.1 The IT SSA

As the SSA for the IT Sector, DHS/NCSD is responsible for coordinating with other government departments and agencies (through the IT GCC) and the private sector (through the IT SCC) to implement and maintain the IT SSP. To implement the actions and activities outlined in the IT SSP, the SSA leverages knowledge, expertise, and guidance from across the IT Sector.

---

[10] Attendees at the annual Quad meeting include members of the IT SCC and GCC, members of the Communications SCC and GCC, and other invited guests and speakers.

NCSD has responsibility for working with public and private IT Sector partners to promote not only the physical, human, and cyber elements of the infrastructure, but also the cybersecurity of all infrastructure sectors as consumers of IT. Table 8-2 outlines NCSD responsibilities.

Table 8-2: NCSD CIKR Partnership Responsibilities

Coordinate Development and Drive Implementation of the IT SSP

- Coordinate efforts to compose and maintain the IT SSP.
- Support implementation of the collaboratively developed risk assessment approach for the IT Sector.
- Coordinate efforts to determine protective measures for the IT Sector.
- Identify R&D requirements and conduct R&D in concert with other government entities, the private sector, and other partners.
- Ensure public and private sector partners are engaged, as early as possible, in the development and revision of the SSP and in planning other CIKR protection initiatives.
- Encourage and promote participation in the IT GCC, IT SCC, and IT-ISAC.
- Support IT-ISAC as the operational information-sharing mechanism for the private sector.

Engage with IT Sector Partners

- Identify relevant public and private sector partners that have a role in securing the IT Sector.
- Develop a plan for regular engagement between NCSD and the public and private IT Sector partners.
- Promote security awareness in the IT Sector.
- Communicate timely, analytical, and useable information, including threat and warning information, specific to the infrastructure and public and private IT Sector partners.
- Identify incentives for the private sector to undertake voluntary efforts to improve security (physical, cyber, and human) and implement the SSP.
- Encourage the use of risk transfer mechanisms, such as contractual arrangements that expand the use of state-of-the-art security practices through market mechanisms.

Engage with Other Government Entities

- Work with the intelligence and law enforcement communities to enhance the collection, assessment, and distribution of cyber-related intelligence to IT Sector partners.
- Solicit input from government entities on IT Sector CIKR protection-related efforts.
- Work with US-CERT to provide cyber alerts, response assistance, and information on remediation measures to public and private sector partners.
- Interact with other SSAs and sectors to identify unique dependencies, interdependencies, relationships, and partnerships across sectors.

8.3.2 IT SCC

The IT SCC enables IT system owners and operators to coordinate on a wide range of sector-specific strategies, policies, activities, and issues related to the protection and resilience of the sector. IT Sector owners and operators are vital contributors to IT SCC implementation-level initiatives. Approximately 50 private sector IT infrastructure and cybersecurity SMEs participated in the ITSRA, representing the commitment of IT Sector owners and operators to enhance the security of the Nation's IT infrastructure. Furthermore, owner and operator companies in the IT SCC have actively engaged in developing the IT Sector's R&D Information Exchange framework. This activity represents the IT Sector owners and operators' support of using consolidated private sector inputs to work collaboratively with government in pursuit of shared R&D goals. Table 8-3 outlines the IT SCC's responsibilities.

Table 8-3: IT SCC CIKR Partnership Responsibilities

Develop and Drive Implementation of the IT SSP
• Participate in the development, review, and enhancement of the IT SSP. • Support the identification and risk assessment of critical IT Sector functions. • Collaborate with NCSD and other public IT Sector partners to identify current and future protective program needs. • Encourage and share advances in security resulting from R&D. • Use IT-ISAC as the focal point for operational information sharing with the private sector.
Engage the IT Public Sector Partners to Promote CIKR Protection
• Identify relevant public sector partners that have a role in securing the IT Sector. • Promote security awareness in the IT Sector.

8.3.3 IT GCC

The IT GCC has responsibility for coordination of strategies, activities, policy, and communications across government entities with a role in securing the IT Sector. Table 8-4 outlines the IT GCC responsibilities.

Table 8-4: IT GCC CIKR Responsibilities

Develop and Facilitate Implementation of the IT SSP
• Lead efforts to develop, review, enhance, and maintain the IT SSP. • Support the identification and risk assessment of critical IT Sector functions. • Collaborate with private IT Sector partners to identify current and future IT Sector protective program needs. • Encourage and share advances in security resulting from R&D.
Engage with IT Private Sector Partners to Promote CIKR Protection
• Identify relevant private sector partners that have a role in the security of the IT Sector. • Participate in the sector partnership model to coordinate with IT Sector partners. • Use available communication tools (e.g., the Homeland Security Information Network Cyber Security Portal, Web site, and telephone hotline) to exchange information with the private sector in relation to the IT Sector. • Promote security awareness in the IT Sector.

8.3.4 Shared Cross-Sector Cybersecurity Responsibilities

Various critical IT Sector functions are consumed by other CIKR sectors and by Federal, State, and local governments. The IT Sector provides the ability to secure IT products and services; however, each sector is individually responsible for the day-to-day operational security of its cyber systems. The IT Sector has an understanding of not only how its products and services are used by consumers, but also an understanding of the security challenges that other sectors face as they use their cyber infrastructure. Public and private IT Sector partners leverage this expertise to assist other CIKR sectors and governments in addressing cybersecurity.[11] CSCSWG provides a forum for cross-sector cybersecurity information exchange. Also, the IT Sector champions

---

[11] In addition to voluntary public and private sector entities in the IT Sector assisting on cross-sector cybersecurity activities, DHS has clear roles and responsibilities for cross-sector cybersecurity. As stated in the 2009 NIPP, "DHS supports the SSAs and other CIKR partners by developing tools and methodologies to assist in identifying cyber assets, systems, and networks, including those that involve multiple sectors. As needed, DHS works with sector representatives to help identify cyber infrastructure within the NIPP risk management framework."

operational information sharing across sectors through US-CERT, the IT-ISAC, and other formal information-sharing methods and bodies during major incidents to promote cross-sector awareness and protection.

8.4 Information Sharing and Protection

Information sharing is a key tool to create situational awareness and effective incident response; therefore, to be useful, information must be timely, relevant, actionable, and labeled so that recipients can glean salient details quickly and efficiently to effectively protect themselves from or respond to incidents. The following descriptions of the categories of information the IT Sector produces, shares, and uses are consistent with information categories identified by the ISAC Council framework:

- **Analytical Product.** An analytical product contains the documented conclusions of public and private SMEs derived by applying threat information against known or perceived vulnerabilities to determine the likelihood of occurrence and the potential consequences. Analytical products include tactical and strategic analysis:

  - **Tactical Analysis** examines factors associated with incidents under investigation or identified vulnerabilities to generate indications and warnings; and

  - **Strategic Analysis** looks beyond individual incidents to consider broader sets of incidents or implications that may indicate threats of potential national importance. Strategic analysis may identify long-term threat and vulnerability trends that could provide advanced warnings of increasing risks, such as emerging attack methods. This type of analytical product gives decisionmakers information they can use to anticipate and prepare for attacks, thus diminishing the potential damage. Strategic analysis also provides a foundation to identify patterns that can support indications and warnings.

- **Data.** Data includes electronic, voice, or printed information routinely provided to trusted members for specified CIKR protection purposes. There are at least three types of data products:

  - **Key Resources Data** is a list of assets and their locations (i.e., in the context of CIKR protection and the building blocks of a critical infrastructure);

  - **Risk Data** pertains to information on the potential consequences to assets, functions, or services at risk, should the incident under study actually occur; and

  - **Vulnerability Data** can be used to assess the degree to which given assets, functions, or services are vulnerable to the threat posed by the potential incident under study.

- **Incident Report.** An incident report should include details on an incident that has occurred, where it occurred, and when it occurred. The impact of the event will be reported as situational awareness.

- **Mitigation Actions.** Mitigation actions are operational practices that individual entities use to enhance the security of their organizations. Examples include application of enterprise solutions to patch management, change management, configuration management, identity management, or procurement of secure systems. Entities may share information with one another or with other sectors about effective enterprise security practices.

- **Needs Requirement.** A needs requirement is any formal request for information (RFI) related to a threat, vulnerability, or incident.

- **Open Source Information.** Open source information is information available for unrestricted distribution.

- **Situational Awareness.** Situational awareness is an assessment of ways an event affects specified assets and infrastructure, including consequential impacts on other infrastructures, missions, and functions. Situational awareness information includes the following:

  - **Advisories** are formal, narrative information bulletins intended to advise the recipient of certain facts, such as new threat information, the occurrence of an incident, or other information.

- **Alerts** are indicators of a change in state. An alert is an advisory of an urgent nature. Alerts can be triggered for numerous reasons, including suspicious activity, aberrations, or abnormalities detected during operations, or other information requiring increased awareness or attention from the sector. Although an advisory notifies and informs, an alert is a call to action.

- **Threat Warning** provides information about an existing or developing threat that may lead to an incident. A warning is specific and actionable rather than merely stating a general concern about a potential event. A warning pertains to imminent events.

In addition to these information-sharing categories, information often has varying degrees of importance and uses. For example, shared information may be time sensitive, or it may be provided for long-term strategic use. Information may also be of varying degrees of sensitivity, such as classified, unclassified, sensitive, proprietary, or open source. In addition, information is often disseminated in a tiered or phased approach based on disclosure constraints related to the sensitivity of the information.

8.4.1 Information Originators and Users

Public and private IT Sector partners focus on building and maintaining trusted relationships to fulfill the IT Sector's goals based on the simple premise that, for information to be useful, it must be shared with the right people at the right time. This section focuses on sharing information between and among the government and individuals who own, operate, and administer the IT infrastructure.

Information sharing is often done voluntarily. Private sector entities typically are not required or mandated to share information. In fact, private sector entities may even face Federal or State government limits on disclosure of sensitive information, and contractual obligations may restrict how and when information is disclosed. Information sharing with the public sector often is complicated by authorities and mandates governing information-sharing activities. For example, government may face difficulty in sharing information because of its sensitivity (e.g., Privacy Act limitation on disclosure of personally identifiable information).

Conversely, the government may be required to disclose information under the Freedom of Information Act (FOIA) or equivalent State disclosure laws. A two-way flow exists between information originators and users. Information users are also information providers and vice versa. Each provides value to the information-sharing cycle. For example, entities that provide information determine how, when, and with whom to share the information and any restrictions that apply. Those who receive it determine how they will use it.

Information sharing in the IT Sector is vital to maintaining situational awareness and addressing the threats to and mitigating the vulnerabilities in the infrastructure. In addition, each of the 18 CIKR sectors is an important node in the information-sharing environment, because they all rely on some combination of the six critical functions of the IT Sector. Cross-sector cyber information sharing is increasingly important as IT continues to permeate national governance structures and economic underpinnings. All CIKR sectors will likely seek cyber-related information in greater frequency and detail as interdependencies become more apparent. This increased reliance on IT infrastructure also means other sectors are important sources of information for comprehensive cyber situational awareness. For this reason, the IT Sector works closely with other CIKR sectors that maintain information-sharing mechanisms for sharing timely and actionable cyber information through the CSCSWG and ISACs.

8.4.2 An Enhanced IT Sector Information-Sharing Framework

Implementing the IT Sector's vision for information sharing may require changes in policy, culture, organization, and technology to create the conditions that facilitate two-way, decentralized, coordinated, and trusted information sharing. Together, public and private sector entities and individuals can build an effective information-sharing environment that accomplishes the following vision:

- Facilitates the flow of information between and among public and private sector partners in a timely, consistent, and predictable manner in a trusted environment, where information is received, disseminated, analyzed, and protected appropriately;

- Fosters a "need to share" culture, where incentives for sharing are realized clearly through value-added products and information;

- Identifies single points for coordinating information and assigns accountability, ensuring that information is being passed to the appropriate individuals;

- Establishes clear roles and responsibilities to help all partners know how they fit in the information-sharing landscape;

- Focuses on organizational levels, ensuring that established communication lines remain intact, even when an individual leaves;

- Articulates incident reporting thresholds to define what constitutes an incident and ensures that a common baseline of corresponding actions exist for each level of severity;

- Features criteria for measuring the effectiveness of information shared and the process for sharing it;

- Considers a mutually shared understanding of each others' information requirements. Public and private sector partners need to clearly state the information they need from each other to carry out their respective CIKR protection activities.

Achieving this vision requires designating organizations as focal points for gathering, analyzing, and disseminating information in a coordinated, reliable, and efficient manner. Defining these primary focal points and clarifying roles and responsibilities assigns accountability for accomplishing the IT Sector's vision for sharing information with the right people at the right time.

8.4.2.1 IT Sector Information-Sharing Initiatives and Mechanisms

Current Initiatives:

- The IT Sector has conduits for sharing policy and operational information. The primary conduits for policy issues are the IT SCC and GCC. Operational information is chiefly exchanged through the IT-ISAC for the private sector and US-CERT and the MS-ISAC for Federal, State, local, and international governments. Identification of key focal points for IT Sector information sharing enables the sector to maintain the flow of information and communication during contingencies.

Policy Mechanisms:

- Consistent with the NIPP, the IT SCC and GCC serve as the primary bodies for exchanging information on policy issues pertinent to the IT Sector. As the strategic leadership for the IT Sector, representatives from both organizations work in close coordination to plan, develop, and coordinate sector-wide programs and initiatives, strategies, and policies. Other partners play a role in policy-related information exchange and provide feeds to and use of information generated by these two bodies. Through information exchange and collaboration, the IT SCC and GCC ensure that sector policies are coordinated and consistent with other national-level initiatives, other infrastructure sectors, SSAs, and other relevant parties, such as PCIS and the Federal Senior Leadership Council, as needed. The sector's participation in the CSCSWG enables IT Sector representatives to identify opportunities to improve sector coordination around cybersecurity issues and topics. The CSCSWG provides a venue for CIKR sector partners to highlight cyber interdependencies and share government and private sector cybersecurity products and findings.

Operational Mechanisms:

- Consistent with the NIPP partnership model and fully endorsed by the IT SCC, the IT-ISAC is the IT Sector's focal point for coordinating the sharing and analysis of operational and strategic private sector information between and among members, as well as with other public and private partners, including Federal, State, and local governments, international entities, and academic institutions. The IT-ISAC serves as a central repository for security-related information about threats, vulnerabilities, and best practices related to physical and cyber events, and it is responsible for the receipt and dissemination of this information to ISAC members. The IT-ISAC also communicates with US-CERT and other sector-specific ISACs. IT-ISAC and US-CERT also developed a Communications Plan to put interactions into operation. US-CERT and the IT-ISAC members meet the first Friday of each month to share information. Together, these capabilities and activities offer members a current and coherent picture of the IT Sector's security.

- US-CERT is a partnership between DHS and the public and private sectors designed to facilitate protection of cyber infrastructure and coordinate the prevention of and response to cyber attacks across the Nation. US-CERT is a 24/7 single point-of-contact for cyber analysis, warning, information sharing, and incident response and recovery for partners, including the IT Sector. US-CERT interacts with Federal departments and agencies, including the IC (through the IC-Incident Response Center), the private sector, academic and research community, State and local governments, the international community, and others to disseminate reasoned and actionable cybersecurity information to the public.

- The MS-ISAC serves as a focal point for information sharing with and among State and local governments. The MS-ISAC is a voluntary and collaborative organization with participation from all 50 States and the District of Columbia. It provides a common mechanism for raising the level of cybersecurity readiness and response in each State and with local governments. The MS-ISAC provides a central resource for gathering information on cyber threats to critical infrastructure from the States and providing two-way sharing of information. In addition, DHS officially has recognized the MS-ISAC as the national center for the States to coordinate cyber readiness and response. The MS-ISAC and US-CERT exchange information regularly to facilitate national coordination of cybersecurity detection, prevention, and response activities.

- The NICC is a 24/7 watch operation center that maintains operational and situational awareness of the Nation's CIKR sectors. The NICC provides a centralized mechanism and process for information sharing and coordination between and among government, SCCs, GCCs, ISACs, and other industry partners. Federal agencies and partners report incidents to the NICC so that the details can be organized and compared against classified known threat information. Through this analysis, the NICC can provide important and timely information about the state of the Nation's CIKR sector through alerts, warnings, and reporting. The NICC provides situational awareness and information sharing during attacks, promotes reconstitution, and provides preparedness support through information sharing. The IT Sector has a cleared representative who is deployed to the NICC during significant incidents to help coordinate response activities across the CIKR community.

- The establishment of State and Local Fusion Centers (SLFC) across the Nation also provides a mechanism for the two-way flow of timely, accurate, actionable, all-hazards information between State and local governments and intelligence and law enforcement communities. During a regional or national event, SLFCs are intended to be central mechanisms for coordinating intelligence, resources, and situational awareness across various levels of governments and with the private sector.

8.4.3 Policies and Procedures for Sharing and Reporting Incidents

The IT Sector's vision for sharing and reporting incidents is listed below:

- Collect, disseminate, and share information along horizontal and vertical paths of an organization and among organizations;

- Communicate in a regular and predictable manner so that information is passed to all appropriate partners and entities are not inadvertently omitted;

- Establish formal policies or procedures to prescribe the flow of information between and among public and private IT Sector partners at all levels;

- Provide intelligence collection and other information requirements to DHS in accordance with the 2009 NIPP;

- Establish and maintain feedback mechanisms to ensure shared information is useful; and

- Develop formal triggers or incident-reporting thresholds to provide consistent guidance to owners and operators for determining when to elevate an event to a higher level or report it to the government.

Fulfilling this vision is critical to institutionalizing the timely and routine dissemination of information that fosters a culture of sharing and minimizes duplication of effort.

Current Initiatives: The IT Sector coordinates with DHS on cyber incidents to promote response and recovery throughout the IT Sector. The primary means by which the IT Sector conducts incident coordination with DHS is through communications between the IT-ISAC and US-CERT through the National Response Framework (NRF) and National Incident Management System (NIMS). During incidents, through the IT-ISAC and US-CERT, the IT Sector interacts with the NICC to share information with the government, implement appropriate prevention and protection programs, and coordinate with their suppliers and CIKR customers to identify and manage potential cascading effects of incident-related disruptions.

IT Sector partners, working through the NSTAC, are also working to enhance existing relationships to promote improved situational awareness capabilities. Members of the IT Sector are working in public-private partnership to develop a National Cyber Incident Response Plan (NCIRP) concept of operations (CONOPS).

Private sector partners are currently developing a CONOPS for a Joint Coordinating Center (JCC) to promote improved situational awareness. The JCC will provide an integrated public-private, 24/7 operational cyber incident detection, prevention, mitigation, and response capability and enable rich, timely, bidirectional sharing of information between the public and private sectors to ensure the ability to detect, protect, mitigate, and respond to cyber threats. A critical building block of the JCC is the newly established NCCIC, which unifies vital IT and Communications Sector operations centers, and thus converges existing incident response mechanisms and better reflects the reality of technological convergence. By incorporating representation from both public and private sector personnel, NCCIC will facilitate timely and effective crisis operations in a significant service disruption or cyber incident. The JCC concept expands beyond IT and Communications sector operations to incorporate Department of Defense entities, carriers, ISPs, representatives from the Banking and Finance and Energy sectors, and international allies.

8.4.4 Procedures for Protecting and Disseminating Sensitive Proprietary Industry Information

The IT Sector's vision for protecting and disseminating industry information is:

- Work in an information-sharing environment that includes rules, policies, and procedures for protecting data to ensure that shared data are protected adequately and consistently across public and private sector organizations;

- Protect sensitive proprietary data from improper disclosure so that business integrity and public confidence are maintained and trust between and among public and private sector partners is fostered; and

- Provide the appropriate operational and technical means to protect and secure data to ensure the integrity, availability, and confidentiality of the information.

Current Initiatives: The IT-ISAC and other information-sharing organizations have implemented strict submission and classification guidance to protect sensitive proprietary data from unwanted disclosure. Membership in the IT-ISAC depends on adherence to these rules, which are enforced through contractual agreements. Members can submit information anonymously or with attributable, identifying information, depending on their preferences or the sensitivity of the information. They also may label submissions designating who can view the information (e.g., the public, IT-ISAC members, or only the ISAC for trending and analysis purposes). Submitted information is protected appropriately according to labeling requirements.

Memorandums of understanding (MOUs) with partners and a consistent labeling framework help ensure that rules and procedures for sharing information are followed. For example, MOUs with other sector ISACs facilitate the exchange of threat and vulnerability data across sectors. This information is vital to assessing IT Sector risk and helps other infrastructure sectors understand risks posed by vulnerabilities in the IT Sector.

Protected Critical Infrastructure Information (PCII) Program: To protect information that is voluntarily shared with the Federal Government, Congress passed the Critical Infrastructure Information Act of 2002 (CII Act), Subtitle B, of the Homeland Security Act of 2002, Public Law 107-296. The purpose of the CII Act is to encourage the private sector to voluntarily submit CII, which often contains proprietary and confidential information, to DHS by protecting CII from disclosure under FOIA and State and local government open records laws, and from use in civil litigation. The CII Act authorizes DHS to receive voluntarily submitted information that qualifies for protection and give it special protection as specified by the CII Act. In accordance with the act, the DHS established the PCII Program to encourage infrastructure owners and operators to share sensitive information voluntarily.

The PCII Program Office receives, evaluates, stores, and shares voluntarily submitted information that qualifies for protection under the legislation. Submissions under the program may be used for various homeland security purposes, including analyzing sector risk and vulnerabilities, securing and protecting systems, and informing response and recovery efforts. PCII is shared with Federal, State, and local governments that are certified to handle PCII and provides a feed into tactical and strategic analysis, vulnerability assessments, alerts, and other products that are shared with various audiences. IT Sector partners use the PCII Program to submit and share information as appropriate.

8.4.5 Access to Classified and Controlled Unclassified Information

The IT Sector's vision for sharing classified and sensitive but unclassified (SBU) government information is:

- Ensure that all key partners, including State and local government officials and private industry personnel, have the requisite clearances for obtaining access to pertinent threat data and analyses provided by the IC;

- Promote uniform policies and procedures governing the designation, handling, and distribution of sensitive data such as law enforcement sensitive (LES), for official use only (FOUO), and controlled unclassified information (CUI); and

- Foster trust by ensuring uniformity and consistency in the level of protection afforded and rules or circumstances for further dissemination, which both help to minimize the risk of compromise and improper disclosure.

Current Initiatives: Security clearances and classifying data enable the Federal Government to protect and restrict access to sensitive or classified information to those with requisite background investigations and a demonstrated need to know. Strict handling and dissemination rules for classified data ensure appropriate and consistent protection and dissemination of that data. Federal departments and agencies have been working with the IT SCC and State and local government officials to grant security clearances to private sector and State and local government officials. The Federal Government, in particular the IC, has been working to develop regular processes for sanitization and production of classified information in a way that allows it to be shared, even if it comes from sensitive methods and sources (e.g., tear-line reports). For example, the DHS Office of Intelligence and Analysis regularly develops and provides periodic classified threat briefings and reports to appropriately cleared IT Sector partners and other CIKR sectors. Finally, the IT Sector plays a leading role in the CUI initiative by providing recommendations and measures to enhance implementation of an effective information-sharing environment across agencies, levels of government, and partners.

8.4.6 Mechanisms for Communicating and Disseminating Information

The IT Sector's vision for information communication and dissemination mechanisms is:

- Ensure automated communication tools can send broadcast messages or alerts to a defined community of users, provide forums for the exchange of information on vulnerabilities, and raise awareness of security issues; and

---

- Have access to and use of tools for information exchange—whether voice, data, and network based—that are secure, robust, survivable, and interoperable.

Current Initiatives: Technology is a key enabler for effective information sharing. It provides partners the means to share and exchange various types of data in real time and across jurisdictional and organizational boundaries, enabling key partners to work from a common operating picture. IT Sector partners use various communications tools to exchange information with each other and with other sectors. These tools facilitate the exchange of information between individuals and larger communities or audiences as needed.

Regular meetings and conference calls also provide a mechanism for exchanging various types of information. The IT-ISAC's Technical Committee exchanges information internally through twice-a-week conference calls, a secure Web site, and encrypted e-mails. The IT-ISAC maintains a Web site for sharing information with the public and internally with its members. A secure portion of its Web site is reserved for ISAC member companies to share information with one other. In addition, the IT-ISAC hosts a daily cyber conference call with US-CERT and the operations centers of other ISACs, as well as a weekly conference call focusing on physical issues with only the operations centers of other ISACs. The Department of Defense and the IC also host numerous conference calls and video teleconferences to share information daily.

IT Sector partners communicate and disseminate information using a secure US-CERT sponsored portal. Through this US-CERT portal, the Federal Government provides Critical Infrastructure Information Notices and other warnings to users to help improve situational awareness. The portal is also a repository of working documents, agendas, white papers, and action items for IT Sector working groups. Participants communicate with one or many other portal users using a secure messaging feature to keep partners informed of strategic or tactical cyber events.

Appendix 1: List of Acronyms and Abbreviations

APEC	Asian-Pacific Economic Cooperation
ARIN	American Registry for Internet Numbers
CAE	Center of Academic Excellence
CAEIAE	National Centers of Academic Excellence in Information Assurance Education
CAE-R	CAE-Research
CEP	Department of Homeland Security Cyber Exercise Program
CEWD	Department of Homeland Security Cyber Education and Workforce Development
CFDI	Critical Foreign Dependencies Initiative
CFIUS	Committee on Foreign Investment in the United States
CII Act	Critical Infrastructure Information Act of 2002
CIIP	Critical Information Infrastructure Protection
CIKR	Critical Infrastructure and Key Resources
CIP	Critical Infrastructure Protection
CIPAC	Critical Infrastructure Partnership Advisory Council
CIP CS	Critical Infrastructure Protection Cyber Security
CNCI	Comprehensive National Cybersecurity Initiative
CONOPS	Concept of Operations
COOP	Continuity of Operations
CNCI	Comprehensive National Cybersecurity Initiative
CS&C	DHS Office of Cybersecurity and Communications
CSCSWG	Cross-Sector Cyber Security Working Group
CSIA IWG	Cyber Security Information Assurance Interagency Working Group
CSSP	Department of Homeland Security Control System Security Program
CUI	Controlled Unclassified Information
DCS	Distributed Control Systems

DDoS	Distributed Denial-of-Service
DHS	Department of Homeland Security
DNI	Director of National Intelligence
DNS	Domain Name System
DoD	Department of Defense
DOJ	Department of Justice
DPA	Defense Production Act
EBK	Essential Body of Knowledge
ECPA	Electronic Communications Privacy Act
EO	Executive Order
FBI	Federal Bureau of Investigation
FIRST	Forum of Incident Response and Security Teams
FOIA	Freedom of Information Act
FOUO	For Official Use Only
G8	The Group of 8
GCC	Government Coordinating Council
GETS	Government Emergency Telecommunications Service
GLBA	Gramm-Leach-Bliley Act
GSA	General Services Administration
gTLD	global Top Level Domain
HITRAC	Homeland Infrastructure Threat and Risk Analysis Center
HSPD	Homeland Security Presidential Directive
I&A	Department of Homeland Security Office of Intelligence and Analysis (I&A)
IC	Intelligence Community
ICANN	International Corporation for Assigned Names and Numbers
ICS	Industrial Control Systems
ICS-CERT	Industrial Control Systems Cyber Emergency Response Team
ICSJWG	Industrial Control System Joint Working Group
IETF	Internet Engineering Task Force
IGF	Internet Governance Forum
IP	Internet Protocol
IP	Department of Homeland Security Office of Infrastructure Protection
ISO	International Organization for Standardization
ISO/IEC	International Organization for Standardization/International Electrotechnical Commission
ISP	Internet Service Provider

IT	Information Technology
IT-ISAC	Information Technology Information Sharing and Analysis Center
ITSRA	Information Technology Sector Risk Assessment
ITU	International Telecommunications Union
IWWN	International Watch and Warning Network
IXP	Internet Exchange Points
JCC	Joint Coordinating Center
LE	Law Enforcement
LES	Law Enforcement Sensitive
MOU	Memorandum of Understanding
MS-ISAC	Multi-State Information Sharing and Analysis Center
NANOG	North American Network Operator's Group
NAP	Network Access Points
NASCIO	National Association of State Chief Information Officers
NCCIC	National Cybersecurity and Communications Coordination Center
NCIRP	National Cyber Incident Response Plan
NCRCG	National Cyber Response Coordination Group
NCS	National Communications System
NCSD	National Cyber Security Division
NICC	National Incident Coordinating Center
NIMS	National Incident Management System
NIPP	National Infrastructure Protection Plan
NIST	National Institute of Standards and Technology
NITRD	Networking and Information Technology Research and Development
NOC	National Operations Center
NRF	National Response Framework
NS/EP	National Security and Emergency Preparedness
NSA	National Security Agency
NSF	National Science Foundation
NSIE	Network Security Information Exchanges
NSP	Network Service Provider
NSP-SEC	Network Service Provider Security forum
NSTAC	National Security Telecommunications Advisory Committee
O&A	Outreach and Awareness
OECD	Organization for Economic Cooperation and Development

OMB	Office of Management and Budget
OMN	Other Mission Needs
OSTP	Office of Science and Technology Policy
PCII	Protected Critical Infrastructure Information
PCIS	Partnership for Critical Infrastructure Security
PCS	Process Control Systems
PDD	Presidential Decision Directive
PN	Public Network
POC	Point of Contact
PSN	Public Switched Network
PSTN	Public Switched Telephone Network
R&D	Research and Development
RFI	Request for Information
RMA	Risk Mitigation Activity
RRA	Risk Response Activity
S&T	Science and Technology
SAR	Sector Annual Report
SBU	Sensitive But Unclassified
SCADA	Supervisory Control and Data Acquisition
SCC	Sector Coordinating Council
SFS	Federal Cyber Service: Scholarship For Service
SHIRA	Strategic Homeland Infrastructure Risk Assessment
SLFC	State and Local Fusion Center
SLGCP	State and Local Government Coordination and Preparedness
SLTTGCC	State, Local, Tribal, and Territorial Government Coordinating Council
SME	Subject Matter Expert
SOX	Sarbanes-Oxley Act
SSA	Sector-Specific Agency
SSP	Sector-Specific Plan
SwA	Department of Homeland Security Software Assurance Program
TLD	Top-Level Domain
TSP	Telecommunications Service Priority
U5	The Usual Five
U.S.	United States
US-CERT	United States Computer Emergency Readiness Team
WAN	Wide Area Network

Appendix 2: Authorities

Key authorities for the IT Sector address the establishment of the IT Sector; its availability, resilience, and security; and provide guidance on sector coordination and specific programs. This appendix provides a brief description of major authorities with relevance to IT Sector CIP activities.

Homeland Security/National Security IT Authorities

The Homeland Security Act of 2002 (November 2002). The Homeland Security Act established the following specific CIKR protection roles and responsibilities for DHS:

- Developing a comprehensive national plan for securing the CIKR of the United States;

- Providing crisis management in response to attacks on critical information systems;

- Providing technical assistance to the private sector and other government entities on emergency recovery plans for failures of critical information systems; and

- Coordinating with other agencies of the Federal Government to provide specific warning information and advice about appropriate protective measures and countermeasures to State, local, and nongovernment organizations.

Homeland Security Presidential Directive 7, Critical Infrastructure Identification, Prioritization, and Protection (December 2003). HSPD-7 establishes a national policy for Federal departments and agencies to identify and prioritize U.S. CIKR and to protect them from attack. HSPD-7 identified Communications and IT as distinct sectors and assigned oversight for both to DHS: NCS serves as the lead DHS agency for the Telecommunications Sector, and NCSD serves as the lead agency for the IT Sector. Specifically, HSPD-7 charges DHS with maintaining an organization—NCSD—to serve as a focal point for the security of cyberspace and facilitate interactions and collaborations between and among Federal departments and agencies, State and local governments, the private sector, academia, and international organizations. The NCSD mission includes analysis, warning, information sharing, vulnerability reduction, mitigation, and aiding national recovery efforts for critical infrastructure information systems. NCSD supports the Department of Justice (DOJ) and other law enforcement agencies in their continuing missions to investigate and prosecute threats to and attacks against cyberspace, to the extent permitted by law. To the extent permitted by law, Federal departments and agencies with cyber expertise, including the Departments of Justice, Commerce, Treasury, Defense, Energy, and State, and the Central Intelligence Agency, will collaborate with and support NCSD in accomplishing its mission.

Intelligence Reform and Terrorism Prevention Act of 2004 (December 2004). This act represents the most dramatic reform to the Nation's intelligence capabilities since the National Security Act of 1947. This authority requires the President to establish an information-sharing environment (ISE) to facilitate sharing terrorism information among all appropriate Federal, State, regional, local, and tribal government and private sector entities through the use of policy guidelines and technologies; to include provisions for privacy and civil liberty rights; to establish programs for the enhancement of public safety communications interoperability; and to recommend that DHS promote the adoption of voluntary national preparedness standards for the private sector. The act and its subsequent authorization legislation established the position of Director of National Intelligence (DNI) and gave the DNI and DNI/Chief Information Officer (CIO) significant additional authorities and responsibilities for the management of the IC and its role in critical infrastructure protection.

Presidential Memorandum for the Heads of Executive Departments and Agencies: Guidelines and Requirements in Support of the Information-Sharing Environment (December 2005). This Presidential memorandum outlines information-sharing authorities and directs executive departments and agencies, in consultation with the program manager for information sharing, to leverage ongoing information-sharing efforts in development of the ISE and to promote a culture of information sharing. In addition, this memorandum provides the following guidelines for the ISE: define common standards for how information is acquired, accessed, shared, and used in the ISE; develop a common framework for sharing information between and among executive departments and agencies and State, local, and tribal governments, law enforcement agencies, and the private sector; standardize procedures for SBU information; facilitate information sharing between executive departments and agencies and foreign partners; and protect the information privacy rights and other legal rights of Americans.

Executive Order (EO) 13311 (as amended by EO 13388), Homeland Security Information Sharing (October 2005). This EO creates an ISE to facilitate the sharing of terrorism information and restructures the Information Sharing Council.

Executive Order 13353, Establishing the President's Board on Safeguarding American's Civil Liberties (August 2004). This EO further strengthens protections for the rights of Americans, including freedoms, civil liberties, and information privacy guaranteed by Federal law, in the effective performance of national security and homeland security functions. Accordingly, this EO establishes the President's Board on Safeguarding Americans' Civil Liberties, chaired by DOJ, which advises the President on information-sharing policy issues.

HSPD-5, Management of Domestic Incidents (February 2003). This directive enhances the United States' ability to manage domestic incidents by establishing a single, comprehensive National Response Plan (now Framework). HSPD-5 places initial responsibility for domestic incident management on State and local authorities, but states that the Federal Government will become involved when State and local resources are overwhelmed or Federal interests are involved. This directive also recognizes the role played by private and nongovernmental sectors in preventing, preparing for, responding to, and recovering from terrorist attacks, major disasters, and other emergencies, and orders the Secretary of Homeland Security to coordinate with private and nongovernmental sectors to ensure adequate planning, equipment, training, and exercise activities, and to promote partnerships to address incident management capabilities.

HSPD-8, National Preparedness (December 2003). This directive establishes policies to strengthen the preparedness of the United States to prevent and respond to threatened or actual domestic terrorist attacks, major disasters, and other emergencies by requiring a national domestic all-hazards preparedness goal, establishing mechanisms for improved delivery of Federal preparedness assistance to State and local governments, and outlining actions to strengthen preparedness capabilities of Federal, State, regional, local, and tribal entities.

HSPD-9, Bio Defense Strategy (April 2004). This directive establishes national policy that prioritizes the protection of critical infrastructure (physical and cyber) from the effects of biological weapons attacks. A biological weapons attack might deny access to essential facilities and response capabilities; therefore, it is necessary to improve the survivability and ensure the continuity and restoration of operations of critical infrastructure sectors following biological weapons attacks. Assessing the vulnerability of this infrastructure—particularly, the medical, public health, food and agriculture, water, energy, and transportation sectors—is the focus of current efforts. DHS, in coordination with other appropriate Federal departments and agencies, leads these efforts, which include developing and deploying biodetection technologies and decontamination methodologies. This HSPD is relevant because human elements of critical IT Sector functions exist. If this human element were affected by a biological attack, cascading effects might occur. For example, if an antivirus vendor organization's campus were affected, the skills and knowledge needed to perform virus definition updates and patching potentially might be unavailable during a crucial time.

HSPD-12, Policy for a Common Identification Standard for Federal Employees and Contractors (August 2004). This directive establishes national policy to enhance security, increase government efficiency, reduce identity fraud, and protect personal privacy by establishing a mandatory, government-wide standard for secure and reliable forms of identification issued by the Federal Government to its employees and contractors (including contractor employees). "Secure and reliable forms of identification" in this directive means identification that: (1) is issued based on sound criteria for verifying an individual employee's identity; (2) is strongly resistant to identity fraud, tampering, counterfeiting, and terrorist exploitation; (3) can be rapidly authenticated electronically; and (4) is issued only by providers whose reliability has been established by an official accreditation process. IT Sector technologies and infrastructure facilitate the implementation of this directive, and future developments in the sector can affect efforts to maintain the common identification standard.

Executive Order (EO) 13231 (as amended by EO 13286 as of February 2003), Critical Infrastructure Protection in the Information Age (October 2001). This EO ensures the protection of information systems for critical infrastructure, including emergency preparedness communications, and the physical assets that support such systems in the information age.

Uniting and Strengthening America by Providing Appropriate Tools Required to Intercept and Obstruct Terrorism (USA PATRIOT) Act of 2001 (October 2001). This act affects companies' IT departments because they must be prepared to provide terrorism-related information to the FBI if subpoenaed.

Export Administration Act of 1979, as amended (EAA), implemented through the Export Administration Regulations (August 2006). The EAA authorizes the Secretary of Commerce to regulate exports of commodities, software, and technology (collectively referred to as "items") based on national security and foreign policy objectives. Under the EAA, controls are placed on export of items based on their technical capabilities and the destination. The EAA currently is lapsed, but the Export Administration Regulations remain in effect through the International Emergency Economic Powers Act (described below), Executive Order 13222, and the Presidential Notice of August 3, 2006.

Exon-Florio Amendment to the Defense Production Act and Executive Orders 11858, 12188, and 12661 (May 1975, January 1980, and December 1988). These provisions authorized the creation of the Committee on Foreign Investment in the United States (CFIUS), which is an inter-agency committee chaired by the Department of the Treasury. The mission of CFIUS is to review and potentially recommend that the President block foreign acquisitions of U.S. companies that threaten to impair national security.

International Emergency Economic Powers Act (IEEPA) (October 1977). This act authorizes the President to engage in a wide variety of activities to deal with an unusual and extraordinary threat to the country's national security, foreign policy, or economy. To trigger authorities under IEEPA, the threat must originate in whole or substantial part from outside the United States, and the President must declare a national emergency for such threat. Using IEEPA, the President has continued the Export Administration Regulation in effect despite the lapse of the EAA, as amended (see above).

National Strategies

The National Strategy for Homeland Security (October 2007). The National Strategy for Homeland Security provides a four-goal framework for national homeland security efforts:

- Prevent and disrupt terrorist attacks;
- Protect the American people, our critical infrastructure, and key resources;

- Respond to and recover from incidents that do occur; and

- Continue to strengthen the foundation to ensure our long-term success.

The *Strategy* focuses on terrorist threats as well as the full range of potential catastrophic events, including manmade and natural disasters, due to their implications for homeland security. As noted within the *Strategy*, many of the Nation's essential and emergency services, as well as our critical infrastructure, rely on the uninterrupted use of the Internet and the communications systems, data, monitoring, and control systems that comprise our cyber infrastructure. A cyber attack could be debilitating to our highly interdependent CIKR and ultimately to our economy and national security. DHS and its private sector partners are working within the NIPP framework to enhance the nation's ability to respond in the event of an attack or major cyber incident.

The National Strategy to Secure Cyberspace (July 2002). This strategy states that a top priority for the Nation is to understand infrastructure interdependencies and improve the physical security of cyber systems and telecommunications. The strategy directs DHS to work with State and local governments to establish strong IT security programs. It also describes the National Cyberspace Security Response System.

National Strategy for the Physical Protection of Critical Infrastructures and Key Assets (February 2003). This national strategy outlines strategic objectives to: identify and assure the physical protection of critical infrastructure and assets; provide timely warning of specific, imminent threats; assure protection of identified infrastructures and assets that face a threat; and assure the protection of infrastructures and assets that may become targets over time by pursuing specific initiatives and enabling a collaborative environment between the public and private sector.

National Counterintelligence Strategy (March 2005). This strategy seeks to ensure that industry is not disadvantaged by foreign intelligence operations and provides appropriate threat information to industry and IT security partners to take appropriate risk mitigation measures. The strategy recognizes that the U.S. strategic response to today's threats requires that the Nation's counterintelligence capabilities need to address technical, cyber, and human threats.

Management and Acquisition of Federal Government Information Technology, Clinger-Cohen Act of 1996 (also known as the Information Technology Management Reform Act) (February 1996). Recognizing the importance of IT for effective government, Congress and the President enacted the Information Technology Management Reform Act and the Federal Acquisition Reform Act. These two acts, together known as the Clinger-Cohen Act, require the heads of Federal agencies to link IT investments to agency accomplishments. The Clinger-Cohen Act also requires that agency heads establish a process to select, manage, and control their IT investments. This act also reformed the way the Federal Government acquires and manages IT through performance-based and results-based management. The law focuses on IT investment management, information resources management, and IT management. It also directs all Federal agencies to use a formal enterprise architecture process. It transferred IT responsibilities from the General Services Administration (GSA) to OMB and further defined the role of an agency's CIO.

Executive Order (EO) 13011, Federal Information Technology (January 2003). This EO outlines a coordinated IT approach that builds on current structures and successful practices to improve Federal Government mission performance and service delivery. It establishes the CIO Council, Government Information Technology Services Board, and Information Technology Resources Board to advise the President in carrying out the responsibilities of the Clinger-Cohen Act.

Memorandum to Heads of Selected Departments and Agencies, Interagency Support for Information Technology (March 1997). This memorandum institutes funds for carrying out EO 13011.

Federal Acquisition Regulation, Part 39, Acquisition of Information Technology (February 2006). This regulation establishes acquisition policies and procedures for acquiring information and IT (excluding national security systems).

E-Government Act of 2002 (January 2002). This act improves electronic Federal Government processes and services promotion and management through the establishment of a Federal CIO at OMB. The act establishes a measurement framework that requires using Internet-based IT to help citizens gain better access to services and information.

The Paperwork Reduction Act of 1995 (May 1995). This act establishes that the OMB Director will develop and oversee the "implementation of policies, principles, standards, and guidelines for information technology functions and activities of the Federal Government" to help enhance agency mission performance.

Federal Information Security Management Act (FISMA) of 2002 (November 2002). This act establishes a framework for the security of the Federal Government's IT by mandating annual audits of Federal Government entities and organizations affiliated with the Federal Government.

Information Technology Audit-Related Authorities

Health Insurance Portability and Accountability Act (HIPAA) (August 1996). Seeks to enhance health insurance coverage portability and continuity; stop health insurance and health care delivery waste, fraud, and abuse; foster medical savings accounts; increase long-term care services and coverage access; and make health insurance administration less complicated. The HIPAA Security Rule establishes minimum standards that safeguard electronic protected health information.

Gramm-Leach-Bliley Act (GLBA) (September 1999). This act establishes the way in which personal information about individuals who obtain financial products or services from financial institutions is shared. Three rules manage personally identifiable information: (1) a financial institution is required to provide a customer with a privacy notice; (2) every financial institution is to create an information security plan; and (3) financial institutions must take precautions to prevent pretexting (i.e., obtaining personally identifiable information without proper authority).

Sarbanes-Oxley Act (SOX) of 2002 (July 2002). This act establishes policies related to corporate governance, the practice of public accounting, and financial disclosure. Section 404 largely affects every company's IT department as it outlines processes for addressing such things as installation of new business applications, application monitoring, and IT system and network security.

Foreign Corrupt Practices Act (FCPA) of 1977 (15 United States Code (U.S.C.) 78dd-1, et seq.) (November 1988). The FCPA seeks to thwart corporate bribery of foreign officials by requiring companies to maintain accurate books, records, and accounts and by requiring publicly traded companies to retain internal accounting control systems.

The Cyber Security Enhancement Act of 2002 (February 2002). The Cyber Security Enhancement Act of 2002 amends Federal computer crime sentencing guidelines, making it possible to issue more appropriate sentences for crimes involving fraud in connection with computers and access to protected information, protected computers, restricted data in interstate or foreign commerce, or involving a computer used by or for the Federal Government.

The Computer Fraud and Abuse Act of 1984 as amended by the Computer Abuse Amendments Act of 1994 (September 1994). Note: Section 1030 was amended on October 26, 2001, by the USA PATRIOT antiterrorism legislation. Section 1030: Fraud and related activity in connection with computers states that whoever, having knowingly accessed a computer without authorization or exceeding authorized access, and by means of such conduct having obtained information that has been determined by the U.S. Government pursuant to an executive order or statute to require protection against unauthorized disclosure for reasons of national defense or foreign relations, or any restricted data, as defined in paragraph y of Section 11 of the Atomic Energy Act of 1954, with reason to believe that such information so obtained could be used to the injury of the United States, or to the advantage of any foreign nation, willfully communicates, delivers, transmits, or causes to be communicated, delivered, or transmitted, or attempts to communicate, deliver, transmit or cause to be communicated, delivered, or transmitted the same to any person not entitled to receive it, or willfully retains the same and fails to deliver it to the officer or employee of the United States entitled to receive it.

National Preparedness and Response Authorities Related to Information Technology Executive Order (EO) 12656, Assignment of Emergency Preparedness Responsibilities (November 1988). This EO delegates NS/EP responsibilities to Federal departments and agencies and instructs agencies to create plans and capabilities that will ensure continuity of essential operations.

Defense Production Act of 1950, as amended (DPA) (October 2009). This act authorizes the President to, among other things, demand that companies accept and give priority to Federal Government contracts that the President "deems necessary or appropriate to promote the national defense." In 2003, the DPA was amended, so that the term "national defense" includes "critical infrastructure protection and restoration." The act authorizes the provision of financial incentives for certain technological development and domestic production.

National Response Framework (January 2008). Emergency Support Function (ESF) #2, Communications, coordinates Federal actions to support temporary NS/EP telecommunications and telecommunications infrastructure restoration. During response efforts, ESF#2 supports all Federal departments and agencies in the procurement and coordination of all NS/EP telecommunications services from the telecommunications and IT industry. The Cyber Security Incident Annex outlines policies, responsibilities, organization, and actions so that the Nation can prepare for, respond to, and recover from nationally significant events related to cyber.

The Robert T. Stafford Disaster Relief and Emergency Assistance (Stafford) Act (October 2000). The Stafford Act establishes the programs and processes for the Federal Government to provide disaster and emergency assistance to States, local governments, tribal nations, individuals, and qualified private nonprofit organizations. The provisions of the Stafford Act cover all hazards including natural disasters and terrorist events. Relevant provisions of the Stafford Act include a process for Governors to request Federal disaster and emergency assistance from the President. Private sector for-profit entities are generally not eligible for Stafford Act assistance.

Information Technology Communications Related Authorities Communications Act of 1934 (June 1934). This act, which established the Federal Communications Commission, regulates interstate and foreign wire or radio communication. The Act also authorizes the President, during times of war or national emergency, to direct priority of communications with certain common carriers, and to suspend or amend regulations applicable to, or direct the closing, use, or control of, certain stations and devices for wireless and wireline communications.

Telecommunications Act of 1996 (January 1996). Title V of the Telecommunications Act, entitled The Communications Decency Act of 1996, criminalizes the intentional electronic transmission of any communication that is obscene or indecent and prohibits the use of a computer network for the purpose of annoying or harassing recipients of messages.

Communications Assistance for Law Enforcement Act (CALEA) (October 1994). CALEA, as it relates to IT, further defines the existing statutory obligation of telecommunications carriers to assist law enforcement in executing electronic surveillance of communications, such as voice over Internet protocol and electronic messaging, according to court order or other lawful authorization. The objective of CALEA implementation is to preserve law enforcement's ability to conduct lawfully authorized electronic surveillance, while preserving public safety, the public's right to privacy, and the telecommunications industry's competitiveness.

Information Technology Privacy Authorities and Information Protection Related Authorities Electronic Communications Privacy Act (ECPA) (October 1986). This act establishes policies for access, interception, use, disclosure, and privacy protection of electronic communications for wire and electronic communications. ECPA prevents the Federal Government from mandating electronic communications disclosure without appropriate procedure.

The National Information Infrastructure Protection Act (October 1996). This act defines "protected information" as "information that has been determined by the U.S. Government pursuant to an EO or statute to require protection against unauthorized disclosure for reasons of national defense or foreign relations, or any restricted data, as defined in paragraph (y)